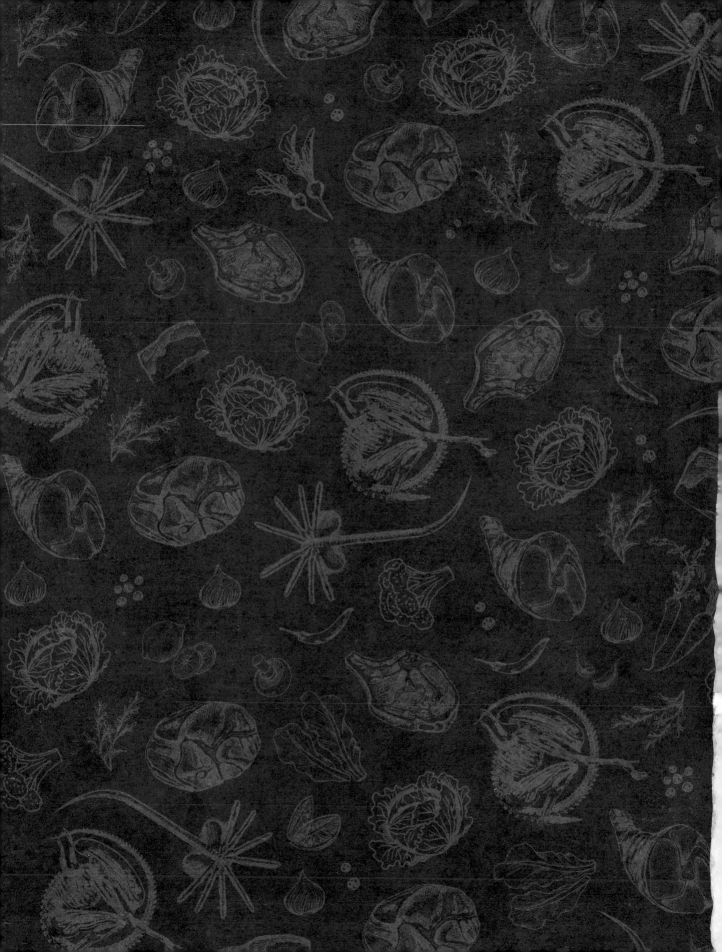

ALIEN

THE OFFICIAL COOKBOOK

ALIEN
THE OFFICIAL COOKBOOK

ISBN: 9781789094831

Published by Titan Books
A division of Titan Publishing Group Ltd.
144 Southwark St.
London
SE1 0UP

FIRST EDITION: NOVEMBER 2020
1 3 5 7 9 10 8 6 4 2

DID YOU ENJOY THIS BOOK?

We love to hear from our readers. Please e-mail us at:
readerfeedback@titanemail.com or write to Reader Feedback at the above address.

To receive advance information, news, competitions, and exclusive offers online,
please sign up for the Titan newsletter on our website: www.titanbooks.com

A CIP catalogue record for this title is available from the British Library.

Printed and bound in China.

ALIEN

THE OFFICIAL COOKBOOK

CHRIS-RACHAEL OSELAND

TITAN BOOKS

CONTENTS

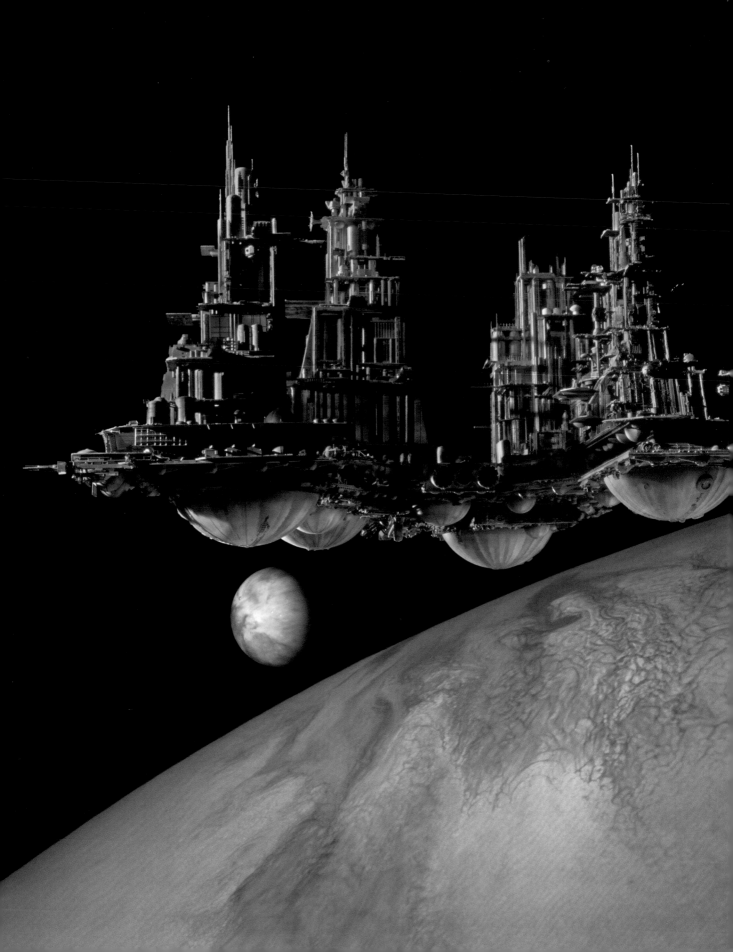

INTRODUCTION

Alien is a film about food.

Maybe *Alien* isn't the first film that occurs to you when you think of gastronomic cinema. But it's no surprise that some of the most startling and subversive events in the franchise happen in and around a dining table.

Not a lot of meals take place on screen in the *Alien* films but those that do are, if you'll pardon the pun, pregnant with tension. In *Alien*, a chestburster erupts from Kane's body during the middle of a peaceful shipboard meal, becoming the catalyst that drives the film to its bloody conclusion. In *Aliens*, Ripley, now wiser, watches the hungry marines of the *Sulaco* with distaste, knowing that their comfort in the social ritual of eating is misguided. Private Frost is correct: "she don't like the cornbread either."

If we don't see much of humans eating in the Alien universe, we certainly see a lot of humans *being* eaten*. The Xenomorph's entire lifecycle revolves around consumption – the larval Xenomorph literally eats its way out of its host's abdomen. The adult Xenomorph lurks through darkened corridors, seeking prey to fuel a biological drive to consume and reproduce. There is a visceral terror in being preyed upon, in being hunted. Alien asks us to revel in the terror of becoming food.

In *Alien*, the nature of the food chain is laid bare. It's about the base processes of eating: hunting, preying, fleeing, surviving. It might not always be food that we would choose to eat, but when has horror or science fiction ever shied away from the delights of gore, blood, and guts?

This book aims to walk the fine line between delicious and horrifying. Learn how to startle and subvert the dining expectations of your guests. Thrill and disgust your friends in equal measure. Devour your way through the Xenomorph's lifecycle… before you become the prey.

*Alien: The Official Cookbook does not condone eating people.

THE ALIEN LIFECYCLE

The Xenomorph goes through a series of discrete life stages before reaching maturity. Xenomorphs have been observed to organise in insectoid, bee-like social structures, with an egg-laying Queen served by many drones in a hive. With lightning-fast reflexes, razor-sharp claws and teeth, a whip-like tail, and acidic blood, even the lowliest drone poses an existential threat to a human. Evidence suggests that Xenomorph eggs can remain dormant for years or even centuries. However, the actual maturation of the Xenomorph occurs rapidly once the larval form has been implanted in a host. A drone can reach maturity in only a few hours.

EGG

The first stage of the Xenomorph lifecycle, eggs are laid in clutches by a Queen, and can lay dormant for extensive periods of time. Eggs are surrounded by a tough, thick membrane to protect the developing facehugger embryo within. A muscular cross-shaped aperture resembling lips sits at the top of the egg and will open when it is time for the facehugger to 'hatch'.

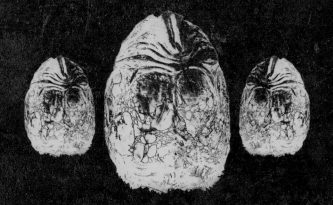

FACEHUGGER

Somewhat resembling a coconut crab, the facehugger runs on eight finger-like legs, which it can use to secure itself to the face of a host. Once secured, it inserts a proboscis through the host's mouth and into their stomach, where it can deposit a Xenomorph embryo. After this is completed, the facehugger dies.

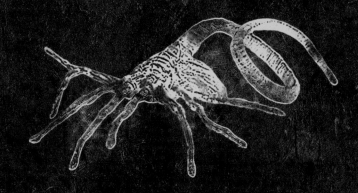

CHESTBURSTER

The chestburster embryo incubates within the host like a parasitic growth. Some scientists have suggested that the DNA of the host exerts some kind of influence over the development of the gestating embryo, with Xenomorphs absorbing some of the phenotypic traits of the gestational host species. Once the chestburster completes gestation, it erupts from the host, killing it, before finding a safe space to moult and grow into a mature drone.

QUEEN

The Xenomorph Queen governs a hive and is the individual responsible for laying eggs. An adult Queen can lay hundreds of eggs in a clutch. She is physically larger and stronger than a drone, but usually rendered immobile due to her massive ovipositor, though she is capable of detaching from this sac in times of distress. Her most distinctive features are her enormous ridged carapace, spiked dorsal spines, and secondary arms, in addition to her gargantuan size. With her chitinous mesoskeleton strong enough to repel automatic gunfire, a single Queen presents an existential threat to the entire human race.

"THIS THING BLED ACID, AND WHO KNOWS WHAT IT'S GONNA DO WHEN IT'S DEAD."

RIPLEY, *ALIEN* (1979)

EGGS

AVOCADO XENOMORPH EGG

MAKES THREE SERVINGS

PREP: 15 MINUTES

DIETARY: VE, V, GF, P*, KE, KP, H

METHOD: EASY

INGREDIENTS

6 large avocados (3 perfectly ripe, 3 over-ripe)

4 fresh limes

¼ cup yellow onion, minced fine

4–6 garlic cloves, minced

¼ cup cilantro, chopped

3 Roma tomatoes, chopped

1 tsp cumin

½ tsp salt

1–2 minced jalapeño peppers, seeds and membrane removed (optional)

Sriracha

Three of your avocados are sacrificial shells. In order to get a pliable green-black egg, the interior will likely be past ripe. Accept this from the start instead of worrying about how you're going to salvage the brown goop inside.

1) Using kitchen shears, very carefully snip an X shape at the top of the three over-ripe avocados. Carefully scoop out the interior flesh. Cut one of the limes into quarters and squeeze one quarter into each emptied shell. Rub the lime juice around the insides to keep them fresh.

2) Cut the remaining limes in half and squeeze the juice into a large bowl. Add the chopped onion, garlic, cilantro, tomatoes, cumin, and salt. If you're using jalapeños, add those now as well. Mix well.

3) Halve your perfectly ripe avocados. Discard the pits and scoop the flesh into your mixing bowl full of ingredients. Mash the avocado into the rest of the guacamole ingredients until everything is well incorporated and at your preferred texture. Some like it smooth, some like it a little chunkier. It's up to you.

4) Hold the edges of the prepared avocado shells back and rub the squeezed limes over the interior edges of the top cut. Carefully spoon guacamole into the avocados, gently packing it down as you go.

5) Before serving, garnish with a few drops of sriracha for blood.

STUFFED FIG
XENOMORPH EGG

MAKES SIX SERVINGS

 PREP: 20 MINUTES

 DIETARY: V, GF, KD

 METHOD: EASY

INGREDIENTS

4 oz creamy goat cheese

4 Tbsp honey

4 Tbsp raspberry balsamic vinegar;

1 cup sweet white wine

24 large dried mission figs

½ tsp kosher salt

Fresh thyme sprigs (optional)

1) Mix the goat cheese with 2 Tbsp of the honey and 2 Tbsp of the raspberry balsamic vinegar until smooth. Put it in the fridge to chill while you work on the next steps. It'll be easier to handle if it's firm.

2) Pour the sweet white wine into a bowl and microwave for 1–2 minutes or until nearly boiling.

3) Cut the stems off the figs. Very carefully snip a small X in the top of each one, going down no more than ⅓ of the fig's body. Drop the figs in the hot wine, stir until they're well covered, and set aside. This hydrates the figs, which plumps them out and makes them easier to stuff. Cover and set aside.

4) Using wet hands, form your goat cheese into little balls. Dip your hands in cold water between balls to keep the goat cheese from sticking. You want to make a little ball of flavored goat cheese that will fit inside a fig without ripping it apart. For most figs that will be about ½–¾ tsp, but use your own best judgment.

5) In a clean bowl, mix the remaining 2 Tbsp honey with the remaining 2 Tbsp raspberry balsamic vinegar. Spread the honey-balsamic mix on the serving plate. The stickiness will help keep the nest of Xenomorph eggs upright.

6) Remove the figs from the wine and dry them on paper towels. Carefully work a pinky finger into the slit in each fig, then slide in your egg-shaped ball of cheese. Pull the sides of the figs up alongside the goat cheese ball to complete the 'just emerging' effect. If the sides won't stick, dab a bit of honey in place. Sprinkle with kosher salt. Garnish with fresh thyme sprigs for that extra organic nest feel.

MATCHA KALE-CRUSTED XENOMORPH EGGS

MAKES FOUR SERVINGS

PREP: 15 MINUTES
COOK: 6 MINUTES

DIETARY: V, GF, KE, KD, H

METHOD: EASY

INGREDIENTS

- 1 tsp white vinegar
- 6 eggs, room temp.
- 1 large bowl ice water
- 12 oz kale chips
- 2 Tbsp matcha, divided
- 1 Tbsp garlic powder
- ½ Tbsp onion powder
- ½ Tbsp black pepper
- ½ tsp salt
- 3 Tbsp olive oil, divided
- 4 cloves garlic, crushed
- 4 packed cups baby spinach
- 2 packed cups baby arugula
- 6 oz herbed goat cheese

We're going to soft boil some eggs so they're organic and runny when you cut into them. An ice bath is the key to stopping the cooking at the right stage. Using room temperature eggs that are at least a few days old will also help make peeling easier. Cold eggs fresh from the grocery store will cling mercilessly to their peels.

1) Bring a pot of water to a boil then turn down to a simmer. Add 1 tsp white vinegar to help with peeling the eggs. Use a slotted spoon to gently lower the eggs into the boiling water. Simmer for 5½ minutes. Use the slotted spoon to transfer your eggs from the boiling water to the ice bath. Set the cold eggs aside. Turn the heat off but do not pour out your hot water.

2) Pulse the kale chips in a food processor until they're a powder. Add the matcha, garlic powder, onion powder, black pepper, and salt. Mix well. It should be a deliciously ominous green.

3) Heat 2 Tbsp of olive oil in a large skillet over medium heat. Add the crushed garlic and cook for 1 minute, stirring frequently. Add the baby spinach and continue stirring until about half wilted. Add the baby arugula and continue stirring until just wilted.

4) Spread the goat cheese into a 4-inch circle in the middle of a plate. From a height of at least 8-12 inches, sprinkle the goat's cheese with matcha and arrange the wilted greens around it.

5) Remove the cooled eggs from the ice bath. Carefully shell each egg. Return the peeled eggs to the hot but no longer boiling water for 30 seconds to warm them back up. Gently dry on a paper towel.

6) Roll the shelled, warmed eggs in the remaining olive oil, then roll the oiled eggs in the kale powder blend. If it doesn't stick, set the egg down and sprinkle the blend on top, letting it rest a bit between each sprinkle. When you're satisfied, gently place the soft-boiled eggs on the bed of goat cheese to create your Xenomorph nest. Before serving, cut one egg in half for full visual effect.

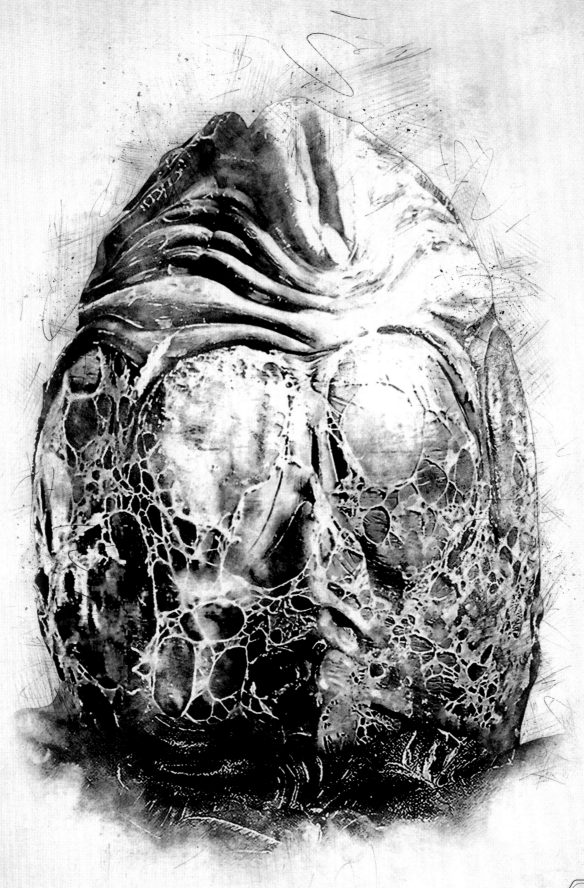

EGGS

HASH BROWN QUICHE NESTS

MAKES SIX TO EIGHT SERVINGS

 PREP: 25 MINUTES
COOK: 25 MINUTES

 DIETARY: GF, V, KD, H

 METHOD: EASY

INGREDIENTS

CRUST:

3 tsp green food coloring, divided

3 cups frozen shredded hash brown potatoes, thawed

1 large egg

½ tsp salt

¼ tsp pepper

⅓ cup shredded Asiago cheese

FILLING:

5 large eggs

½ tsp paprika

¼ tsp salt

¼ tsp pepper

½ cup roasted red bell peppers, chopped

3 green onions chopped thin - both white and green

½ cup fresh baby spinach, thinly sliced

⅔ cup shredded Cheddar Jack cheese

1 cup Easy Restaurant-Style Salsa (see page 128) (optional)

1) Preheat oven to 400°F. Butter a 12-hole muffin pan.

2) Start by making the crust. First, mix 2 tsp of green food coloring and ½ cup water. Soak the thawed hash browns in the green water for 10 minutes. Drain and gently squeeze dry.

3) In another bowl, whisk together the remaining 1 tsp green food coloring, egg, salt, and pepper until they are well blended. Mix in the shredded Asiago cheese. Finally, mix in the green tinted potato shreds, tossing gently until everything is well coated.

4) To make the crusts, press about ¼ cup of the potato mixture into each muffin hole. Really cram it tight onto the bottom, then press it up the sides. Try to make it form 4 spikes, like a Xenomorph egg that has cracked open.

5) Bake your shells for 15–18 minutes, or until a pale golden brown. Don't overbake; they're going back in the oven soon!

6) While the crusts bake, make the quiche filling. Beat the eggs with the paprika, salt, and pepper, then mix in the roasted peppers, baby spinach, white ends of the spring onions, half the green spring onion, and the cheddar jack cheese.

7) Carefully spoon the filling into the baked hash brown cups. Bake for 6–8 minutes, or until a knife inserted into the middle comes out clean.

8) Serve as-is, or optionally with a dollop of spicy, chunky salsa in the middle of each egg cup to hint at something bloody.

ARTICHOKE AND SPINACH DIP

MAKES THREE SERVINGS

 PREP: 10 MINUTES
COOK: 2 HOURS

 DIETARY: V, K, KD, H

 METHOD: EASY

INGREDIENTS

FILLING:

1 cup cream cheese, softened

1 cup sour cream

½ cup mayonnaise

6–8 garlic cloves, minced

2 cups shredded mozzarella

½ cup shredded gruyere

½ cup shredded Parmesan

*10 oz frozen chopped spinach,
    thawed and chopped*

*14 oz jar artichoke hearts,
    drained and chopped*

2–2½ Tbsp red food coloring
    (optional)

BOWLS:

3 large whole artichokes

*1 large lemon,
    cut into quarters*

1) Dump all the filling ingredients into a 4-quart crockpot. Mix well, put the lid on, and set it to low. After 1 hour, remove the lid and thoroughly stir. Put the lid back on and let it cook for another hour.

2) While the dip cooks, prepare your artichoke bowls. Cut the stem on the bottom so the artichokes stand upright. Cut off the top ¼ of the pointy end. Pry the leaves loose and cut out the hard inner choke. Scrape the interior clean, then rub each artichoke interior thoroughly with a lemon quarter.

3) When the dip is ready, spoon it into the hollowed artichokes. If you want, you can try to selectively pluck some leaves to make it look more like the egg is splitting open. If you want a reddish, gory look, add some food coloring to the dip and mix to evenly distribute before spooning into the artichokes.

SPICED ALIEN TEA EGGS

MAKES SIX SERVINGS

PREP: 20 MINUTES
SOAKING: 4 HOURS
COOK: 15 MINUTES

DIETARY: V, GF*, P*, KE*, KP

METHOD: MODERATE

INGREDIENTS

12 eggs, room temp.

Ice water bath

2 inches fresh ginger, sliced

2 star anise

1 cinnamon stick

2 bay leaves

4 Tbsp loose black tea

1 tsp whole peppercorns

4 Tbsp soy sauce

2 Tbsp brown sugar

1 tsp salt

2 Tbsp rice wine vinegar

2 tsp green food coloring

6 short cucumbers

Sriracha (to taste)

Once the tea eggs are fully soaked, the goal is to mount the eggs inside the cucumber pedestals so it looks like you have a freshly laid nest (of visually impressive vegetarian-friendly appetizers.) For full flavor, dip bites of the egg and cucumber into the broth when eating.

1) Add the eggs to a pot of cold water. Bring it to a boil. Let it boil for 10 minutes, then use a slotted spoon to remove the eggs. Immediately place them in an ice bath to stop them from cooking.

2) In another pan, mix 2 cups of water with the fresh ginger, star anise, cinnamon stick, bay leaves, loose tea, whole peppercorns, soy sauce, brown sugar, and salt. Bring it to a boil and let it simmer for 10 minutes while the eggs cook.

3) Add the rice wine vinegar, green food coloring, and 1 cup of the ice water to the tea blend. Give it a good stir. Pour the tea blend into a bowl or pan large enough to fit all of the eggs.

4) Hold each cooled egg in a tea towel. Using the back of a spoon, gently tap the shell. You want to crack the shell in many places without entirely breaking it. Lots of little cracks, but nothing ripped through.

5) Place each cracked egg into the tea blend and add just enough water to the tea blend to submerge all the eggs. Let them soak for at least 4 hours, preferably overnight. The longer they soak, the stronger the flavor and the darker the coloration. When you peel the eggs they will have a dark spiderweb pattern against the white of the egg.

6) Cut the cucumbers in half. Each curved end will be the top while the cut side will be the bottom. Cut an X into the curved end of the cucumber about 3–4 inches deep. Very carefully use a paring knife to hollow the white interior out of the cut cucumber tops. The goal here is to create a little nook where the eggs can rest while also having dark green petals that stretch up most of the side of the eggs. Carefully cut the bottom of the cucumber stumps so they're different heights. This gives your creepy nest a more 3D feel, as if the eggs were freshly laid.

7) When you're satisfied that your cucumbers are properly hollowed, peel an egg and gently ease it into the cucumber hollow. Repeat for all the eggs and cucumber halves. Arrange the nest of eggs in a wide, deep platter or bowl.

8) Spoon the leftover broth over the eggs and cucumbers. Let it pool at the bottom to give it that organic, freshly laid look. If you'd like, you can finish each egg by adding a drop of sriracha to the top of each egg.

ROASTED RADISH EGGS
IN BODY-MELTING CITRUS SAUCE

MAKES FOUR SERVINGS

 PREP: 10 MINUTES
COOK: 30-35 MINUTES

 DIETARY: VE, V, GF, P, KE, KP, H

 METHOD: EASY

INGREDIENTS

12 small or 6 medium
Watermelon Radishes
 (about 2 lbs)

¼ cup olive oil

1 tsp kosher salt

1 tsp smoked paprika

½ tsp garlic powder

½ tsp onion powder

½ tsp black pepper

Body-Melting Citrus Sauce
 (see page 126)

Roasted radishes taste a lot like a tangier roasted potato. The watermelon radish variety is available in winter at upscale groceries. It has a green and white exterior and a deep, organic pink interior, making it perfect for experimentation with Alien Eggs!

1) Preheat your oven to 400°F.

2) Wash the radishes, then cut off the stem end so they sit flat. Use a sharp knife to cut a deep X into the top of the radishes about ¾ of the way down. Don't cut all the way through.

3) Mix the olive oil and all the spices in a large bowl. Rub the mix into the radishes, working some into the X cut if possible. Arrange the radishes on a metal baking sheet, flat side down and X side up.

4) Roast for 30-35 minutes, or until the exterior is crispy and the radishes are baked through and creamy soft in the middle.

5) While the radishes bake, make your body-melthing citrus sauce (see page 126).

5) When the radishes are roasted, pour ¼ cup of the marinade onto the serving plate. Arrange your roasted radishes on top so it looks like a menacing nest of freshly opened eggs. You can either drizzle more the sauce over the eggs or leave it as a dipping sauce on the side.

STUFFED ACORN SQUASH

MAKES FOUR SERVINGS

 PREP: 20 MINUTES
COOK: 30 MINUTES

 DIETARY: GF, P

 METHOD: MODERATE

INGREDIENTS

4 medium green-black
acorn squash

4 Tbsp olive oil, divided

1 lb chorizo

1 lb ground beef or pork

1 large yellow onion, diced

6 cloves garlic, minced

2 Tbsp butter

1 cup tart apple
(such as granny smith), diced

2 packed cups baby spinach

1 Tbsp fresh rosemary leaves
(ripped from stem & chopped)

1 Tbsp fresh thyme leaves
(ripped from stem & chopped)

½ tsp salt

1 tsp black pepper

¼ tsp paprika

3 cups mozzarella (optional)

1) Preheat your oven to 400°F.

2) Cut the tops off the acorn squash and set them aside. Reserve the tops for later. Scoop out the interior seeds and strings. Rub the interior of each squash and the bottom of the tops with olive oil. Lay the squash and tops on a baking sheet cut side down and bake for 20 minutes. Remove the tops and continue baking for another 5 minutes. Take the squash out of the oven and let them rest.

3) In a large skillet, brown the chorizo and ground meat. When the meat is cooked through, set it aside. You should still have some lovely juices in the pan.

4) Return the pan to the heat. If there's not much juice left, add 1 Tbsp olive oil. Add the chopped onion and cook until lightly browned, 4–5 minutes. Add the garlic and cook for another 2–3 minutes or until browned. Mix the onion into the bowl of meat and return the pan to the heat.

5) Melt the butter and add the apple. Cook over medium heat until the apple is golden brown and soft, but not totally mushy. Mix this into the onion and meat mixture and return the pan a final time to the heat.

6) Add another Tbsp of oil to the pan. Throw in the spinach, rosemary, and thyme. Cook, stirring frequently, until the spinach is wilted. Add the spinach to the meat mixture. Top it all off with salt, pepper, and paprika. Knead the mixture like you're making bread. You want everything well mixed together. Form the filling into four equal-sized balls and gently stuff a ball into each of the four squashes.

7) Switch the oven to broil. Return the squash to the oven, stuffed side up. Do not include the tops. Broil for 6–8 minutes or until the tops are toasty but not burned. Optionally, you can add ¾ cup of mozzarella over the top of each squash half. This will give it a gooey, organic look as well as cheesy deliciousness. Just return it to the broiler for 60–90 seconds, or until the cheese is melted but not browned.

8) Place the squash tops on top of each squash, a little askew, or cut them into quarters so it looks like the lips of the egg just opening up.

RETRO BOLOGNA QUICHE CUPS

MAKES SIX SERVINGS

 PREP: 15 MINUTES
COOK: 10 MINUTES

 DIETARY: N/A

 METHOD: EASY

INGREDIENTS

4 slices bacon

4 large eggs

4 cloves garlic

½ small onion, chopped small

2 Tbsp chopped fresh chives

¼ tsp salt

¼ tsp pepper

⅛ tsp Worcestershire sauce

½ cup shredded mozzarella

18 slices bologna lunchmeat

12 toothpicks

6 leaves boston bibb lettuce
(optional)

Since *Alien* came out in 1979, it only seems fitting to honor it with a suitably retro 1970s-inspired recipe.

1) Preheat oven to 400°F. Fry the bacon until crispy, chop, and set aside. Use the bacon grease to lubricate six holes of a muffin tin.

2) Beat together your eggs, garlic, onion, chives, salt, pepper, chopped bacon, Worcestershire, and mozzarella cheese.

3) You'll use three slices of bologna for each finished 'egg'. Push one slice into a muffin tin hole and press it up against the sides. Press in a second slice and try to make the upper edges curl in a different pattern, then do the same with a third slice. Repeat with each of the muffin holes until the bologna is used up. Spoon the filling into the bologna cups.

4) Pinch the two sides of the top edges of the bologna closed and hold in place with a toothpick. Repeat with the opposite side. You should now have a toothpick X at the top of each bologna cup. Don't seal it completely closed; some moisture needs to escape while they cook.

5) Bake for 8–10 minutes, or until the bologna is lightly crispy and the filling is set. It's ready when a knife slid into the interior egg filling comes out clean. Let the bologna eggs cool in the muffin tin for 5 minutes before handling.

6) Put a piece of Boston Bibb lettuce in a round ramekin. Gently slide the 'eggs' out of the muffin tin. Place one 'egg' in each ramekin and pull the lettuce up around it. Remove the toothpicks. The bologna will open a little, like a Xenomorph egg cracking.

PREP: 20 MINUTES
COOK: 40 MINUTES

DIETARY: KP*, H*

METHOD: EASY

INGREDIENTS

1 lb mild ground Italian chicken sausage

1 cup butter, divided

1 small yellow onion, peeled and chopped (about ¾ cup)

6 cloves garlic

2 celery stalks, chopped into ¼ inch slices

2 Tbsp chopped fresh or 1½ tsp dried sage leaves

1 Tbsp chopped fresh or 1 tsp dried thyme leaves

½ Tbsp chopped fresh or ½ tsp dried rosemary leaves

2 tsp salt

½ tsp pepper

1 egg

3–3½ cups chicken broth, divided

¼ cup dried cranberries

9 cups dried bread cubes

12 large Granny Smith or other green apples

1) Preheat oven to 350°F.

2) Put a large skillet over medium-high heat. Cook the sausage until fully browned and cooked through. Pour it in a bowl and set aside.

3) In the same skillet, add 1 Tbsp butter. Fry the onion, garlic, and celery for 3–4 minutes, until soft but not cooked through. Add to the bowl with the ground sausage, along with the sage, thyme, rosemary, salt, and pepper, egg, 2½ cup chicken broth, and cranberries, and mix it all into an ugly slurry.

4) Finally add the bread cubes. Mix well so everything is well combined and set aside, to give the bread a little time to absorb the moisture. If the stuffing seems too dry, add another ¼ cup of broth.

5) Now it's time to prepare the apples! Cut the tops off all the apples and set the tops aside. Use a melon baller to scoop out the apple's insides. Leave a wall about ¾ inch thick. Spoon stuffing into your apples, taking care not to break them.

6) Arrange a nest of apples in a cake pan, cut side up. Pour ¼ cup broth over the top of the apples, and another ¼ cup into the bottom of the pan. Bake for 30 minutes, until the apples are soft but not mushy.

7) While the apples are baking, use a round cookie cutter or sharp knife to remove the stem from the apple tops. Carefully cut an X shape in the middle of the apples. Don't go all the way to the edges. You want to leave at least 1½ inch of space around the edges. Rub the apple tops with butter. Arrange them skin side down on a cookie sheet. Add them to the oven during the last 15 minutes of cooking your apples.

8) Remove the stuffed apples and their tops and let them cool for at least 10 minutes, so you can handle them without burning yourself.

9) Put the tops onto the apples. Gently peel the four corners of the X back to create the effect of a Xenomorph egg cracking open.

STUFFED GREEN PEPPER
WITH GARLIC KALE
MAKES FOUR SERVINGS

 PREP: 20 MINUTES
COOK: 30 MINUTES

 DIETARY: GF, KE*, KD*, H

 METHOD: EASY

INGREDIENTS

BELL PEPPERS:

4 large green bell peppers

½ cup uncooked
   long grain rice

1 lb 80/20 ground beef

1 medium yellow onion,
   chopped

4 garlic cloves, minced

1 Tbsp oregano

½ tsp salt

¼ tsp pepper

15 oz can tomato sauce

4 Tbsp tomato paste

GARLIC KALE:

2 bunches kale

3 Tbsp olive oil

4 cloves garlic, thinly sliced

¼ tsp onion powder

¼ tsp paprika

¼ tsp black pepper

½ tsp kosher salt

Choose bell peppers that are able to stand up on their own. You'll thank me later. The kale lets you hide the fact that the bottom of the peppers aren't really egg shaped.

1) Preheat oven to 375°F.

2) Use a sharp knife to cut the stem out of each bell pepper. Cut 4 little slits around the stem in an X shape, no more than ½ inch deep. This will make it easier to remove the core and veins. Once the peppers are emptied and deveined, set them aside.

3) Bring 2 cups of water to a boil. Add the long grain rice and boil for 10 minutes, until softened. The rice will not be done yet; it will finish cooking while in the peppers. Drain the softened rice and put it in a bowl.

4) Meanwhile, brown the ground beef. When it's fully cooked through, add it to the same bowl as the parboiled rice. Don't drain the fat.

5) Return the pan and pan juices to the heat. Add the onion and cook for 5–7 minutes, or until translucent and starting to brown at the edges. Add the garlic and cook for another 2–3 minutes, or until it starts to turn golden brown. Scrape the contents of the pan into the bowl with the meat and rice. Try to get all the drippings. Add the oregano, salt, and pepper. Mix well.

6) Add the tomato sauce and keep mixing until everything is well blended. It will be wet and saucy. Carefully spoon the filling into the peppers until they're very full but not bursting. Smear 1 Tbsp of tomato paste over the exposed meat of each stuffed pepper, and just under the cut edges.

7) Arrange the peppers in an 8 x 8 inch cake pan so they're helping each other stand upright while baking. Bake for 25–30 minutes or until the meat is cooked through and the tomato sauce topping has started to blacken a little.

8) While the peppers bake, prepare the kale. Remove the ribs and stems of the kale and chop the leaves crosswise. Add 3 Tbsp olive oil to a large skillet. Toss in the garlic, onion powder, paprika, and black pepper. Sautee for 1–2 minutes over medium heat.

9) Add the chopped kale in batches. As each handful wilts down enough to add more, keep piling it in. Once all the kale is in the skillet, keep cooking, stirring often, for 7–10 minutes, or until it's wilted down to your preferred texture. Put a lid on, turn down to low, and keep warm until the peppers are done.

10) Place the cooked peppers on a serving plate and arrange the kale around the bottoms so it looks like eggs resting in a nest. Sprinkle the kale with kosher salt and serve to your willing victims.

CHEESE-STUFFED MUSHROOM EGGS

MAKES FOUR SERVINGS

 PREP: 10 MINUTES
COOK: 30-35 MINUTES

 DIETARY: V, GF, KE, KD, H

 METHOD: EASY

INGREDIENTS

1 lb cremini or baby
portabella mushrooms

5 oz garlic and herb cheese

1 tsp red food coloring
(optional)

⅓ cup grated Parmesan
cheese

Butter

1) Preheat oven to 350°F.

2) Gently pop the stems off your mushrooms and discard.

3) With a hand mixer, beat the garlic and herb cheese, and optionally beat in the food coloring. Spoon the whipped cheese into the mushrooms until the filling barely crests the top.

4) Press the cheese-filled top of the mushrooms into the grated Parmesan cheese. This creates a nice crust on top. Arrange your mushrooms in a 9 x13 inch baking dish, cheese side up.

5) Slide a sharp knife against a stick of butter. Cut an X into the cheese stuffing. The goal here is to make sure the baking cheese 'cracks' in the shape you want. Try not to cut the mushrooms themselves.

6) Bake for 30–35 minutes, or until the tops are golden and puffy with a hint of a pink X in the middle.

"I ADMIRE ITS PURITY. A SURVIVOR...
UNCLOUDED BY CONSCIENCE, REMORSE,
OR DELUSIONS OF MORALITY"

ASH, *ALIEN* (1979)

SAUSAGE-STUFFED BAKED ARTICHOKE

MAKES SIX SERVINGS

 PREP: 20 MINUTES
COOK: 1 ½ HOURS

 DIETARY: N/A

 METHOD: EASY

INGREDIENTS

1 lb spicy ground
  Italian sausage

½ cup + 2 Tbsp grated
  Parmesan cheese, divided

½ cup Italian seasoned
  bread crumbs

½ teaspoon kosher salt

½ teaspoon ground
  black pepper

6 garlic cloves, minced

6 large artichokes

1 cup white wine

2 bay leaves

1 large sprig rosemary

olive oil

1) Preheat the oven to 375°F.

2) Mix the sausage, ½ cup of Parmesan cheese, breadcrumbs, salt, pepper, and garlic until everything is well combined. Set aside.

3) To prep the artichokes, pull off the hard outer leaves. Trim the bottom of the artichokes so your nest of alien eggs can stand upright. After that, cut off the top ¼ of the artichoke, leaving it flat on top. Gently use your fingers to pry the leaves open. Use a melon baller or a sharp knife to cut out the hard inner 'choke' part of the artichoke. Keep loosening the leaves so there's room to stuff filling between them.

4) Divide the meat stuffing into 6 equal parts. Taking one ball and one prepared artichoke, start by stuffing the hollowed middle, then try to cram a little meat in between as many of the leaves as possible.

5) Once all the artichokes are stuffed, place them in a dutch oven. They should be in a single layer, stem down, stuffing up, like a nest of eggs full of ominous potential. Pour in 1 cup of white wine. Top the pot off with water until the liquid comes halfway up the artichokes - probably around 3 cups. Don't over fill it. Sneak the bay leaves and rosemary sprig below the water line.

6) Sprinkle the top of the artichokes with more salt and pepper, then sprinkle the remaining 2 Tbsp of Parmesan cheese over the tops. Lightly drizzle them with olive oil. Put the lid on your dutch oven (or cover your large pot with foil). Tuck it into the oven for 1½ hours. Check on the artichokes after 60 minutes. They'll be done when a single leaf pulls out easily and the meat stuffing is cooked through.

7) To serve, scoop an artichoke into a bowl and spoon ¼ cup of the cooking liquid over the top.

POPCORN BALL ALIEN EGGS

MAKES TWELVE EGGS

PREP: 30 MINUTES
COOK: 5 MINUTES

DIETARY: V*, KO*, H, GF

METHOD: MODERATE

INGREDIENTS

18 cups popped popcorn

6 Tbsp salted butter

18 oz caramel candies, unwrapped

½ tsp red food coloring (optional)

4 cups mini marshmallows

8 cups chocolate candy melts

6 cups green candy melts

1 pink or white icing pen

12 popsicle or craft sticks

1) Pour the popcorn in a strainer to sift out the unpopped kernels.

2) Grab a huge stockpot. Melt the butter over medium heat. Toss the caramel candies into the melted butter and stir gently until they melt into a smooth caramel. Add the red food coloring (optional) and half the marshmallows and keep stirring until the marshmallows melt into the caramel. (The red food coloring helps give the interior of the popcorn balls a more fleshy color.)

3) Remove the stockpot from the heat. Mix in the popcorn and the remaining mini marshmallows.

4) Using buttered hands, shape about 1½ cups of popcorn into a large egg. Tap the bottom onto a flat surface so it stands upright on its own. When all 12 are finished, use a buttered kitchen knife to slice an X into the top ¼ of each egg. Carefully pull the four sides of the X open so it looks like your eggs are hatching.

5) Shove a popsicle stick into the middle of each X. Arrange your proto-nest on a sheet of waxed paper.

6) Microwave the chocolate candy melts in a large microwave safe bowl, stirring every 15 seconds. When the mix is smooth and liquid, grab one egg by the popsicle stick and roll it in the chocolate until completely coated. Set it aside and roll the rest of the eggs. If the eggs are still too lumpy feel free to roll them in the chocolate a second time.

7) Once the chocolate coating has hardened, microwave the green candy melts, stirring every 15 seconds until the mix is completely smooth. Dip the eggs into the green chocolate. Don't try to get it into the top X, and don't stress if your coverage is a little spotty. The eggs are supposed to look rough and organic.

8) Once the eggs dry, pull out the popsicle sticks. Depending on how suggestively gory you want to make them, use either your pink or white icing pen to outline the interior of the X.

GINGER, AVOCADO & COCONUT MOUSSE

MAKES FOUR SERVINGS

 PREP: 10 MINUTES

 DIETARY: VE, V, GF, P, KP, H

 METHOD: EASY

INGREDIENTS

1 cup coconut cream

2 large ripe avocados
  (about 1 cup of flesh, mashed)

2 Tbsp or agave syrup

1 ½ Tbsp ginger paste

½ tsp vanilla extract

⅛ tsp salt

12 drops green food coloring
  (optional)

4 large strawberries

If you can't find coconut cream, try two cans of whole fat coconut milk. Put them in the fridge overnight then scoop the solid cream off the surface. The remaining liquid is a great substitute for water when making rice or quinoa.

1) Dump all the ingredients other than the strawberries into a large bowl. Beat on high for 2–3 minutes. You want to not only get everything blended, but also whip in some air. If you have a stand mixer, use the balloon attachment and let it beat air into the mix on high for a solid 5 minutes. Feel free to add food coloring if you'd like your eggs to be a darker green.

2) Spoon the mousse into 4 stemless wine glasses. The more egg-shaped the better. Chill the mousse for at least 2 hours, or up to 4 days in the fridge.

3) Before serving, cut the stems off the strawberries. Carefully slice an X from the pointy end down almost to the base. Pry the strawberries open so they look like petals and lay them on top of the mousse. Use one finger to ever so slightly push it down into the surface of the mousse so it looks like the pink inner petals of an alien egg are splayed open. Alternatively, serve the mousse in large shot glasses. Fill each one about ⅔ with mousse and tuck the cut strawberry into the middle. Push it down into the mousse without any green goo getting inside or rising up over the top, so it looks like the seams of the egg are just opening up.

FACEHUGGERS

KALE-CRUSTED BAKED POTATO

WITH CHEESY FINGERS

MAKES FOUR SERVINGS

 PREP: 30 MINUTES
COOK: 1½ HOURS

 DIETARY: GF, V*, KD*, H

 METHOD: MODERATE

INGREDIENTS

CHEESE STRAWS:

2 sheets puff pastry, thawed
  in the fridge overnight

2 cups white cheddar
  jack cheese

1 cup grated Parmesan

1 tsp white pepper

½ tsp salt

1 tsp red pepper flakes
  (optional)

POTATOES:

12 oz kale chips

4 tsp kosher salt

2 tsp pepper

4 Tbsp olive oil

4 large russet potatoes

ASSEMBLY:

9 slices cooked bacon
  (optional)

8 Tbsp butter

8 Tbsp sour cream

Since *Alien* came out in 1979, it only seems fitting to honor it with a suitably retro 1970s-inspired recipe.

CRUST

1) Preheat the oven to 375°F.

2) Flatten the puff pastry. Mix the cheeses, white pepper, salt, and (optional) red pepper flakes. Spread half the mix on each sheet of puff pastry. Use a rolling pin to press the cheese mix into the pastry.

3) Using a pizza cutter, slice each sheet into 12 long 'fingers.' Twist each finger before laying it on a parchment paper-lined baking sheet. To add to the facehugger effect, pinch the pastry every 2–3 inches to create 'knuckles' and bend it slightly so it will bake in a come-hither shape.

4) Bake for 10–15 minutes, or until each finger is lightly puffed. Flip and bake for another 2 minutes. Don't overbake or the cheese will burn.

POTATOES

1) Preheat the oven to 375°F.

2) Blitz the kale chips in a food processor until they form a powder. Mix the salt and pepper into the kale powder and set aside.

3) Scrub the potatoes to remove any dirt. Dry the potatoes, then thoroughly rub them with oil. Use a fork to poke a few holes in

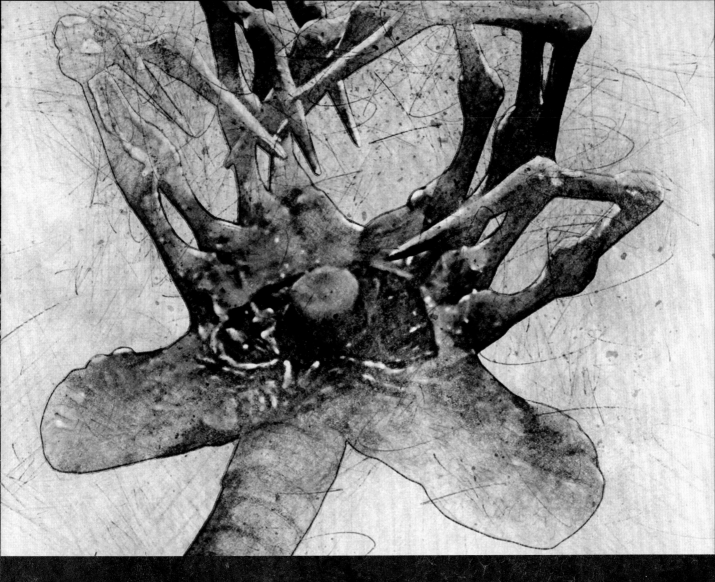

each side. Gently roll the oiled potatoes in the kale powder mix. Make sure to cover the entire surface as thoroughly as possible.

4) Bake for 60 – 80 minutes (depending on the size of your potatoes). They're done when the sides are soft and a knife slides through with no resistance.

ASSEMBLY

1) When the potatoes have cooled enough to handle, gently tap the bottom against a flat surface until it's able to stand upright. If it's determined to fall over, don't stress. They'll still look and taste amazing.

2) Once you've determined a 'top' side, snip that familiar X shape to create a bursting egg. Immediately add 2 Tbsp of butter to each potato then smear 1–2 Tbsp sour cream into the wound to give the potatoes that wet, organic look.

3) Carefully arrange the shorter cheese stick fingers so they look like they're reaching up out of the potato egg. Serve your masterpiece with extra loaded baked potato fixings of your choice (salsa makes a great blood substitute). If you're using bacon, wind the bacon on the 'floor' of your serving platter to give it the organic look of sloppy bits leftover from dead hosts.

AVOCADO & BACON STUFFED DEVILED ALIEN TEA EGGS

MAKES SIX SERVINGS

 PREP: 15 MINUTES

 DIETARY: GF, P, KE

 METHOD: EASY

INGREDIENTS

6 slices bacon

12 tea eggs (spiced alien tea eggs, see page 24)

3 ripe avocados

3 Tbsp lime juice

3 garlic cloves, minced

1 tsp chili powder

1 tsp salt

1 tsp black pepper

Paprika (for sprinkling)

1) Cut bacon into long, thin strips lengthwise before cooking. Fry the strips, using a pair of silicon tongs and a spoon to shape the bacon into crooked fingers as it cooks. Crumble any failed fingers and set aside.

2) Peel the tea eggs. Cut an X shape into the top of each egg, far enough down that you can see the yolk. Carefully scoop the yolk out with a teaspoon, without ripping the egg white.

3) Put all the egg yolks in a large bowl. Cut the avocados in half, remove the pits, and scoop the flesh into the bowl with the yolks. Add the lime juice, minced garlic, chili powder, salt, and pepper. Using a hand mixer, beat the mixture smooth. Add in any crumbled bacon bits that weren't good enough to be facehugger fingers.

4) Very carefully spoon the filling into the eggs. If you're feeling fancy, load it into a pastry bag and pipe it in.

5) Arrange your eggs in a creepy nest. You can put them on a bed of salad, cooked kale, or other greens if you'd like to make the nest even more organic. When you're satisfied with the look, sprinkle paprika on top of each egg. Arrange 4 of the bacon 'fingers' around the edges so it looks like they're trying to claw their way out of the eggs and serve. Save any extra filling for sandwiches.

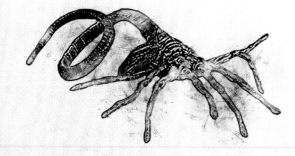

FACEHUGGER CORDON BLEU

OVER POTATO SKINS

MAKES FOUR SERVINGS

INGREDIENTS

POTATO SKINS:

8 Russet baking potatoes

3 Tbsp olive oil

3 Tbsp butter

3 tsp kosher salt

2 tsp garlic powder

1 tsp onion powder

½ tsp fresh ground black pepper

CHICKEN CORDON-BLEU:

6 slices ham

4 slices Emmental cheese

4 slices Gouda cheese

4 thick chicken breasts

½ cup flour

1 tsp salt

1 tsp pepper

2 tsp paprika

2 eggs

2 Tbsp water

1 cup panko breadcrumbs

DIJON CREAM SAUCE:

2 Tbsp butter

2 Tbsp flour

1 ¼ cups whole milk

2 Tbsp Dijon mustard

¼ cup grated Parmesan cheese

 PREP: 30 MINUTES
COOK: 45 MINUTES

 DIETARY: N/A

 METHOD: COMPLEX

The potato skins in this recipe will sub in for the facehugger's fingers and tail. You'll need to start them first, so everything finishes cooking around the same time. From 8 potatoes, you should have 16 potato skins. Each chicken breast will use 4 potato skins to create a facehugger.

POTATO SKINS

1) Preheat the oven to 400°F.

2) Poke all the potatoes with a fork. Rub them with olive oil and microwave for 7–9 minutes, until cooked through. Let them cool for a few minutes.

3) When the potatoes have cooled enough to handle, cut them in half lengthwise and scoop out their guts. Leave about ½ inch of potato around the skins. You can save the scooped interiors for mashed potatoes.

4) Melt the butter and mix in the salt, pepper, onion powder, and garlic powder. Use a pastry brush to liberally paint the inside and outside of the skins with the butter mixture.

5) Arrange the potato skins in a single layer on a baking sheet and set them aside until the chicken is ready to bake.

CHICKEN CORDON BLEU

1) Lay down a piece of ham. Top it with two slices of Emmental, letting them overlap a little. Add another layer of ham, then a layer of Gouda,

also overlapping. Repeat, layering ham, Emmental, ham, Gouda until you run out of ham. Squish your ham stack together. Cut into four vertical strips and set it aside.

2) Set up a little dredging station. In a shallow bowl, sift together flour, salt, pepper, and paprika. In a second bowl, whisk eggs and water, then in a third bowl pour the panko breadcrumbs. Set the three bowls in a row.

3) Cut a slit along the top center of your chicken breasts. They should look just as suggestive as the pink underside of a facehugger. Dredge the chicken in the seasoned flour, then dip it in the whisked eggs. Finally, dredge it in the panko breadcrumbs. Ensure the breadcrumbs coat the entire surface.

4) Lay the breaded chicken breasts on a parchment paper-lined baking sheet. Nestle one ham stack into the slit. Repeat for the other 3 breasts.

5) Put both the potato skins and the chicken into the oven. Bake for 15 minutes. Flip the potato skins over. Rotate the chicken 180° degrees. Bake for another 15 minutes (30 minutes total). The chicken should be golden brown with oozing cheese in the middle and the skins should be crispy. If either needs more time in the oven, cook for another 5 minutes.

DIJON CREAM SAUCE

1) Melt the butter over a medium heat. When it's frothy, add the flour and whisk it together. Stir constantly as it cooks for the next 3–4 minutes. Pour in half the milk and whisk until there are no lumps. Add the rest of the milk and the Dijon mustard and Parmesan cheese. Cook for another 3–5 minutes, whisking constantly. It'll thicken slightly. Turn off the heat and set it aside. It will

1) Lay a chicken breast in the middle of a plate. Cut one potato skin into 8 strips, and a second into 6. Tuck two of the smallest strips at the top of the chicken breast, for the outer probing fingers. Tuck three of the longer strips on the left, then three more on the right, to form 'fingers'. Use more strips to extend the fingers by pinching the ends together to form a 'knuckle'. If the fingers curl a little, that's perfect.

2) Cut one potato skin in half and flatten both halves with your hand. Tuck the edges of the flattened halves under the chicken, behind the rear legs. This makes the facehugger's rump flaps.

3) For the tail, cut a fourth potato skin into three slices, lengthways. Cut the outer thirds in half, leaving you with 5 strips total. To make the tail, place the widest center strip under the narrow end of the chicken breast, then pinch one of the remaining strips to end-to-end, thickest to narrowest. Feel free to curl the tail around a little.

4) Repeat with the other 3 chicken breasts so your entire party of 4 each have their own facehugger taunting them over dinner. To serve, pour some of the Dijon sauce into the middle of each chicken breast slit.

OVEN-ROASTED BOK CHOY FACEHUGGERS

MAKES FOUR SERVINGS

 PREP: 15 MINUTES
COOK: 15 MINUTES

 DIETARY: V, VE, P*, KE, GF*, KP, H

 METHOD: EASY

INGREDIENTS

BOK CHOY:

*2 large baby bok choy/
 pak choi*

2 Tbsp olive oil

1 tsp kosher salt

*1 tsp fresh cracked black
 pepper*

SAUCE:

1 tsp olive oil

1 shallot, peeled and minced

4 cloves garlic, minced

1 Tbsp low sodium soy sauce

1 Tbsp brown sugar

1 tsp fish sauce (optional)

1 tsp sriracha (optional)

½ tsp sesame oil

1) Preheat oven to 400°F. Line a baking sheet with parchment paper.

2) Cut the bok choy in half, lengthwise. Lay them cut side up on the parchment paper. Drizzle the tops with olive oil then sprinkle them with salt and pepper. Bake for about 15 minutes, or until the leaves are soft and the tops are slightly caramelized.

3) While the bok choy bakes, make the sauce. Pour the olive oil in a skillet over medium-high heat. Cook the shallots for 4–5 minutes, stirring often. Add the garlic and continue cooking for another 2–3 minutes. Turn heat down to medium. Add the brown sugar, soy sauce, and fish sauce (if using). Add sriracha to taste. Stir well, cooking until the brown sugar melts. Turn off the heat and mix in the sesame oil.

4) Remove the bok choy from the oven and carefully turn each one cut-side down. Leave the stem fully intact but cut through the leaves down to where they join the stem. Turn the bok choy back over, cut side up. Carefully tug the freshly sliced leaves to make two long 'fingers' pointing upward. Now pull out three individual leaves on each side (six total) to create the 'fingers' of the facehugger. Bunch the remaining leaves together and pull them into an S shape to create the tail. When all the bok choy is baked and arranged into facehuggers, finish them off by drizzling the cut end with the sauce.

FACEHUGGER CHEESEBALL
WITH PULL-APART BODY
MAKES FOUR SERVINGS

INGREDIENTS

CHEESE BALL:

3 cups shredded
   mozzarella cheese

1 cup shredded
   cheddar cheese

16 oz cream cheese, softened

¾ cup olive oil

2 tsp crushed red pepper

1 tsp dried basil

1 tsp dried oregano

1 tsp garlic powder

1 tsp kosher salt

½ tsp black pepper

1 cup marinara sauce
   (see page 129)

1 cup pepperoni slices

PULL-APART BREAD:

1 refrigerated ball of
   pizza crust dough

8–10 balls of aluminum foil,
   of varying sizes

1 Tbsp olive oil

1 Tbsp salted butter, melted

1 tsp garlic powder

½ tsp onion powder

1) Put all the cheese ball ingredients except the marinara and pepperoni slices into a food processor and pulse until smooth. Scrape the mixture out with a rubber spatula, wrap in plastic and refrigerate for at least an hour.

2) Preheat the oven to 450°F. Line a baking sheet with parchment paper.

3) Roll and stretch the pizza dough until it's shaped like a pear. Stretch the narrow end of the pear so it becomes a long tail. Use your hands to flatten the pear. This will be your facehugger's body. Don't worry about details because it's going to be covered by the cheeseball.

4) Use kitchen shears to snip eight 2-inch pieces along the sides of your pear, four on each side. Gently tug these out to form the facehugger 'fingers'. Pinch the dough in 3 places to make the finger joints. Coil each finger over a small ball of aluminum foil to create the curled-up shape.

5) Use a chopstick to press deep indentations into the tail every inch along its length. Put a foil ball under the rump end so the tail rises up before it falls. Use another ball under the very end of the tail so it looks like it's coiled to strike.

6) Mix the olive oil, melted butter, garlic, and onion powder and brush it over the entire surface. Bake for 12–14 minutes, or until the crust is baked through and a light golden brown.

7) Remove from oven and allow to cool. Leave the aluminum balls in place so the bread will harden into the right shape. When the crust is completely cool and the cheeseball has set, it's time to merge the two! Get a bowl of warm water and a kitchen towel, because this will get messy.

8) First, line the body of the facehugger with slightly overlapping pepperoni slices. This prevents the bread from getting too soggy and adds visual impact. With damp hands, smush the cheese ball onto the body of the facehugger. Make it roughly pear shaped. Leave a visible rim of pepperoni on the outside.

9) Use your fingers to carve a line in the middle of the cheese ball, from 'head' to 'tail'. Gently spread the crease open, making a deeper well near the 'tail' end. Line the crease with pepperoni slices, then fill it with the marinara. About an inch out from the center crease, use chopsticks to carve two shallower creases either side of the center line. Slide in a row of slightly overlapping pepperoni slices to create parallel red curves. Use a chopstick to add as much or as little detail as you like. Remove the aluminum foil balls right before serving.

PREP: 20 MINUTES
CHILL: 1 HOUR
COOK: 15 MINUTES

DIETARY: N/A

METHOD: MODERATE

ENCOURAGE YOUR GUESTS TO RIP OFF THE FACEHUGGER'S LIMBS AND TAIL AND DINE ON ITS INTERIOR. IT'S ONLY FAIR.

VINTAGE SHRIMP FACEHUGGER

MAKES FOUR SERVINGS

 PREP: 20 MINUTES
COOK: 40 MINUTES

 DIETARY: N/A

 METHOD: MODERATE

INGREDIENTS

CURRY SAUCE:

6 Tbsp butter

½ cup all-purpose flour

2 tsp curry powder

1 tsp salt

½ tsp pepper

2¼ cups hot chicken stock

¼ cup pineapple juice

SHRIMP & BANANAS:

4 firm yellow bananas

2 Tbsp butter, melted

½ tsp salt

1 lb fresh shrimp,

2 Tbsp olive oil

½ tsp salt

¼ tsp pepper

2 Tbsp pineapple juice

2 cups cooked rice, hot

CURRY SAUCE

1) Melt the butter in a saucepan over medium heat. When it's frothy, add the flour, curry powder, salt, and pepper and stir until smooth. Cook for 3–4 minutes. Pour in the stock ¼ cup at a time, whisking it completely smooth between additions. When all the stock is incorporated, add the pineapple juice. Continue cooking over medium heat, stirring constantly, for another 5–8 minutes, or until the sauce is smooth and thickened. Take it off the heat and set it aside.

SHRIMP AND BANANAS

1) Preheat the oven to 375°F.

2) Cut the bananas in half, lengthwise. Line a baking sheet with parchment paper and arrange the bananas in a single layer, cut side down. Use a pastry brush to paint them with melted butter.

3) Bake for 15–18 minutes, or until the bananas are fork tender. Remove from the oven and set aside.

4) Peel and devein the shrimp. Pour the olive oil into a large skillet and place it over medium-high heat. When the oil shimmers, toss in the shrimp in a single layer, giving them plenty of room to breathe. It's fine if you have to work in multiple batches. Cook the shrimp for 2 minutes, stirring often. Add the salt, pepper, and pineapple juice and continue cooking for another 2 minutes, or until the shrimp curl inward and turn pink with a white sheen. Remove them from the heat and cover while you prepare the rest of the meal.

ASSEMBLY

1) Arrange two banana halves so they look like they're pointing forward at the front of a platter. Arrange the rest into legs. You need three legs on each side. Fill the space between the bananas with rice.

2) Pour the Curry Sauce over the edges of the rice, where they meet the bananas. Arrange the shrimp over the rice so they form ridges like the ones you see on the backs of face huggers. Serve?

NESTING PEPPERS

MAKES EIGHT SERVINGS

PREP: 20 MINUTES
COOK: 25 MINUTES

DIETARY: V, GF, KE, KD, H

METHOD: MODERATE

INGREDIENTS

4 cups cream cheese, softened

4 Tbsp paprika

6 garlic cloves, crushed and minced

2 tsp salt

1 tsp fresh ground black pepper

4 cups shredded cheddar cheese

7–8 large red bell peppers

4 green jalapeños

4 scotch bonnet/ habanero peppers

4 Thai red chili peppers

Handling the peppers will leave potentially dangerous oils on your hands, so wear gloves and take care to avoid touching your face or body while handling them. If you don't have any gloves, be very, very careful to wash your hands at least twice after handling the peppers, and do not touch your eyes, mouth, or anywhere sensitive. This recipe can be halved if you don't have 8 brave souls willing to eat so many hot peppers!

1) Preheat the oven to 350°F.

2) Beat the softened cream cheese until it's smooth. Beat in the paprika, minced garlic, salt, and pepper. When that's well combined, mix in the shredded cheddar cheese. Set aside.

3) Cut 4 red bell peppers and all the other peppers in half and remove the seeds and stems. The remaining bell peppers will become the facehugger's limbs and tail.

4) Fill the 8 red pepper halves with cream cheese. Gently push a jalapeño half into the middle of the filled pepper, scooping out any overflowing cheese filling and using it to stuff the jalapeño half. Repeat the process with a scotch bonnet half in the jalapeño, then the Thai red chili in the scotch bonnet, stuffing each pepper with cheese filling before placing the next.

5) Bake the facehuggers on a parchment-lined baking tray, cheese-side up, for 20–25 minutes, then broil them for another 3–4 minutes until the cheese is bubbly and the tops barely start to darken. Keep a watchful eye so they don't burn!

6) While they bake, cut the remaining red bell peppers into long slices. When plating the facehuggers, hook 4 slices onto each side of each facehugger. Break 8 more slices in half and arrange them next to the bottom of the legs to create additional joints in the 'fingers'. Serve with android-blood inspired tumblers of milk to combat the heat of the peppers.

INVASION OF POT PIES

MAKES SIX SERVINGS

PREP: 20 MINUTES
COOK: 1 HOUR 15 MINUTES

DIETARY: GF*, H*

METHOD: MODERATE

INGREDIENTS

4 Tbsp unsalted butter + extra for greasing

1 medium yellow onion, diced

4 garlic cloves, minced

⅓ cup all-purpose flour

½ cup white wine

1½ cups chicken broth

1 cup heavy cream

2 tsp kosher salt

½ tsp fresh ground black pepper

2 tsp fresh thyme leaves (about 3–4 sprigs)

1 tsp fresh rosemary leaves (about 1–2 sprigs)

1 tsp fresh sage leaves (about 5–6 leaves)

2 lbs yellow potatoes, cut in 1½ inch dice

2 lbs carrots, peeled and cut in 1½ inch dice

½ lb green beans, cut into 2-inch chunks

1½ lbs shredded cooked chicken (rotisserie or leftovers)

1 cup frozen peas

8 refrigerated pie crusts (or your own favorite recipe)

Don't substitute milk in place of cream in this recipe. Cream can boil without curdling or breaking, while milk cannot. If you're using fresh seasonings, you can tie them up with a little kitchen twine and dump the whole bundle in as-is with no stripping or chopping. A lot of the leaves will fall off, seasoning the broth, but the stems will be easy to fish out later with a pair of tongs. If you prefer, you can strip all the herbs from the stems and finely chop them instead.

1) In a stockpot or Dutch oven, melt the butter over medium heat until it's nice and frothy. Add the onion and cook for 5 minutes, stirring occasionally. Add the garlic and cook for another 3–4 minutes, or until the onions and garlic are golden but not brown.

2) Add the flour and cook for 3 minutes, stirring constantly. Add the wine and stir until completely absorbed. Add the chicken broth and stir until there are no flour lumps. Add the cream.

3) Add the salt and pepper as well as the herbs and give it all a good stir. Add the carrots and potatoes. Turn the heat down to low, cover, and let the veggies simmer in the broth for 20 minutes, stirring occasionally.

4) Add the green beans and shredded chicken. Continue to simmer for another 5 minutes. Remove the lid and add the peas. Continue to simmer for another 5 minutes or until the peas are cooked through. Use a pair of tongs to remove the bundle of herbs (if using). Turn off the heat.

5) Preheat the oven to 375°F. It's time to make some facehuggers! Butter both the inside and outside of six oven-proof ramekins. Cover a baking sheet with parchment paper and put the ramekins on it. Fill each ramekin to the brim with the chicken filling.

6) Roll out the refrigerated pie crusts. Using one pie crust, cut a pear shape just barely larger than each ramekin. You want it to hang over the sides a bit. This makes the base of the body. To make the middle of the body (the central 'abdomen'), cut a narrow, cone-like triangle shape about $\frac{1}{4}$ the length of your ramekin. Use the remaining pieces of the single crust dough to create a long tail. Squeeze the end of the tail and the base of the abdomen together. Use a chopstick to press indentations in the whole length, about 1 inch apart. Set aside until after you've attached the fingers. Repeat this for all 6 facehugger pies, using 6 of the 8 pie crusts.

7) Use the 2 additional pieces of pie crust to make the 'fingers.' Divide the remaining crust into 48 similar-sized balls, then roll each ball of pie crust into long, thin sausages. Attach 4 on each side of the pies, evenly spaced along the front half of the body. Pinch and smooth the dough to attach it to the base. They'll naturally fall over the side of the ramekin. That's why you have the parchment paper underneath. Gently pinch the fingers in 3 places to make the joints.

8) Lay each cone-shaped abdomen crust over the center of each base crust. It should cover the joins where you attached the fingers. Gently use the back of a spoon to smooth the pie crust so it attaches to the bottom layer. Wrap the tail around the body of the ramekin, keeping it underneath where the fingers overhang. Cut vent slits on the body outside the abdomen and between the fingers. Cover the 'fingers' with foil so they don't burn.

9) Bake 25 minutes. Remove the foil and continue baking for another 5–7 minutes, or until the bodies and limbs are all a nice golden brown.

CHERRY PIE TARTS
WITH FACEHUGGER FINGERS

MAKES TWELVE SERVINGS

PREP: 30 MINUTES
CHILL: 2 HOURS
COOK: 25 MINUTES

DIETARY: V, KD

METHOD: MODERATE

INGREDIENTS

GREEN PIE CRUST:

¼ cup cold vodka

2 Tbsp cold water

2 Tbsp green food coloring +
  2 drops blue

2½ cups all-purpose flour

1 tsp salt

¾ cup cold, unsalted butter,
  grated or cut into
  small cubes

½ cup chilled solid
  vegetable shortening,
  cut into cubes

CHERRY PIE FILLING:

4 cups fresh or
  frozen tart cherries

1½ cups sugar

¼ cup cornstarch

¼ tsp salt

¼ tsp almond extract

2 Tbsp butter

FINISHING TOUCHES:

Pocky sticks
  (or similar long, thin cookies)

¼ cup chocolate melts

12 vanilla wafers

The goal here is to make the pies look like eggs that have just opened, and a baby facehugger is clawing its way out for the very first time.

CRUST

1) Mix the vodka, water, and food coloring. Put them in the fridge until they're nice and cold.

2) Whisk together the flour and salt. Use a pair of butter knives to mix the cold butter into the flour. When that's mostly combined, use the knives to mix in the vegetable shortening until the mixture resembles coarse crumbs. Sprinkle the cold vodka mixture over the top. Fold it into the crumbs until you achieve a tacky dough.

3) Divide the dough into two balls. Flatten the balls, wrap them in plastic, and chill them in the freezer for one hour or in the fridge overnight (or up to 2 days before using).

4) When you're ready to make your tarts, first aggressively butter a 12-hole muffin tin. Roll the pie crust out to ⅛–inch thickness. Cut the pie crust into squares large enough to overlap the muffin holes. You want to have four flaps folded open on the pan itself. Gently push your green square pie crust into the well buttered holes. Arrange them so that the pie crust corners don't touch. Remember, you want those petals peeking out! Cover the muffin tin with plastic and pop it back in the fridge to rest for an hour. This will prevent shrinkage.

5) After an hour, remove the plastic, prick holes at the bottom of each tart crust with a fork, and bake at 425°F for 15–20 minutes, or until both the top and bottom are golden brown. Check after 15 minutes and keep checking every few minutes until they're done. Once the tart crusts are nice and baked, set them aside.

PIE FILLING

1) Place cherries in a medium saucepan over medium heat. Cover and let them cook for about 10 minutes, stirring occasionally, until they leak considerable juice.

2) While the cherries cook, whisk together the sugar, corn starch, and salt in another bowl. Sprinkle the mix over the cherries and stir until it's all incorporated. Keep sprinkling and stirring until you run out of powdery goodness. When everything's mixed in, keep stirring until the mix thickens. When it reaches the consistency you like, stir in the almond extract and take it off the heat.

ASSEMBLY

1) Spoon the pie filling into the green tart crusts. Use the back of the spoon to drag the filling up the sides of the petals so they look sticky and organic.

2) Microwave the chocolate melts for 15 seconds. Stir, microwave for another 15 seconds, and stir again. Repeat until the chocolate melts smoothly.

3) Break the finger cookies in half and dip the broken ends in the chocolate. Use it to glue them back together at an angle, so they look like fingers crawling out. Prop the chocolate ends of the finger cookies inside the cherry filling and the uncoated ends outside. You can have as few as four of them peeking out or go for the full 8. When you're satisfied with the legs, lay a vanilla wafer on top of the filling and press down gently, and repeat for all the pies. Randomize it a little so it looks like facehuggers are climbing out of the nest at their own special pace.

"WHAT'S THE MATTER? THE FOOD AIN'T THAT BAD..."

PARKER, *ALIEN* (1979)

SWEET FACEHUGGER BREADSTICKS

MAKES SIX SERVINGS

PREP: 20 MINUTES
COOK: 15 MINUTES

DIETARY: V, VE, KP, H

METHOD: EASY

INGREDIENTS

2 packages refrigerated bread dough

Nonstick cooking spray

2 Tbsp honey (optional)

½ cup sugar

Bloody salted caramel sauce

(see page 127)

1) Gently flour a rectangle of bread dough and roll it out slightly. Cut it into 16 equally spaced slices. A pizza cutter is perfect for this.

2) Roll 12 pieces of dough into sausages. Use a butter knife to gently press lines every ⅛ inch along the entire length. Facehuggers have ridges, after all. Set the rest of the dough aside.

3) Liberally grease the bottoms of 12 small brioche cups, the inside of the muffin tins, the top surface of the muffin tins and 12 small balls of aluminum foil. Put a greased ball of foil in all the exterior muffin holes and line up four greased brioche cups on either side of the muffin tin.

4) Put one inch of a dough sausage on the surface of the muffin tin. Gently drape the dough inward so it coils around the ball of foil. Loop it at least once, then give it a little wiggle and put the 'head' squarely in the middle of the nearest overturned and greased brioche cup.

5) Take the remaining 4 slices of dough and cut each into four long strands, lengthwise. Cut those in half at the middle, to create 8 strands per dough slice.

6) Lift the head of your facehugger. Arrange four strips underneath the head so they fall down the natural grooves of the brioche cups on either side, creating eight little limbs. Gently pinch the limbs to create knuckles. Use a chopstick to press an upside-down V shape into the 'face' end of your facehugger. Press a small line between each of the limbs. Liberally sprinkle the whole thing with sugar. Optionally, add a line of honey into the V you made earlier to give it a bit more definition.

7) Bake the breadsticks according to the package directions. (Usually 375°F for 12–16 minutes but check your dough package!) Remove from the oven when they're golden brown. Let them cool for at least 10 minutes so you can lift them out of the muffin tins completely intact. Serve with a side of bloody salted caramel as a dipping sauce.

PEAR AND CARDAMOM UPSIDE-DOWN CAKE

MAKES TWELVE SERVINGS

PREP: 20 MINUTES
COOK: 45 MINUTES

 DIETARY: V, KD, H

 METHOD: EASY

INGREDIENTS

¾ cup butter, room
   temperature, divided
   (+ extra for greasing)

¾ cup packed brown sugar

4 firm Anjou pears

1½ cups all-purpose flour

2 tsp baking powder

¼ tsp salt

¾ tsp cardamom powder

¾ cup white sugar

2 eggs

1¼ tsp vanilla

¼ tsp almond extract

½ cup milk

1) Preheat oven to 350°F. Liberally coat a 9-inch round cake pan with butter.

2) Melt 4 Tbsp butter in a large skillet over medium heat, stirring occasionally. When the butter is foamy and barely starting to brown, add the sugar. Cook for 3–4 minutes, stirring often, until all the sugar has melted into the butter and you've achieved a smooth and creamy caramel. Pour the caramel into the pan and set it aside.

3) Peel all four pears, core them and cut them in half. The biggest pear half will serve as the middle of the facehugger body. Put it cut side down in the middle of the pan. Now pick two small pear halves. Cut the narrow ends off, leaving only the bulbs. Place these on either side of the bottom of the center pear to create the facehugger's rump flaps. Use the spare parts you just cut off to form a triangle at the bottom. These will be the start of the facehugger's tail.

4) Slice the remaining pear halves into strips lengthways and arrange them neatly into four 'legs' on either side of the central pear. Neatly arrange any remaining pear slices from the base of the tail curling outward along the side of a pan, overlapping slightly, for ¼ of the circumference

of the pan. This creates the rest of the tail. Set the pear and caramel pan aside while you mix the batter.

5) Whisk the flour, baking powder, salt, and cardamom together. In a large mixing bowl, cream the rest of the butter with the granulated sugar. Add the eggs, one at a time, and continue beating. Scrape down and add the vanilla and almond extracts. Mix in half the dry ingredients, then half the milk. Continue mixing and add in the rest of the dry then the rest of the milk. Continue beating until everything is well blended and the batter is fluffy.

6) Carefully spoon the cake batter over the pears. With wet hands, carefully press it down. The goal here is not to disturb your hard work in arranging the pear slices. Bake at 350°F for 40 minutes, or until a cake tester comes out clean.

7) Let the cake cool in the pan for 10 minutes. Gently loosen the sides with a thin rubber spatula. Hold a plate face-down over the pan and flip the whole thing over, then remove to pan to reveal the upside-down cake. If some of the pear slices don't behave, poke them back into place and scrape any remaining caramel in the pan over the areas you had to repair.

CHESTBURSTERS

RED PEPPER QUICHE
WITH SAUSAGE CHESTBURSTER

MAKES FOUR TO SIX SERVINGS

PREP: 20 MINUTES
COOK: 1 HOUR 10 MINUTES

DIETARY: N/A

METHOD: EASY

INGREDIENTS

1 premade pie crust

1 Tbsp olive oil

½ yellow onion, diced

4 garlic cloves, minced

6 stalks asparagus, chopped

10 oz spinach

8–10 fresh basil leaves

6 large eggs

1 cup heavy cream

1 tsp salt

½ tsp fresh ground pepper

½ cup shredded cheddar cheese

1 cup tightly packed roasted
    red bell peppers, drained
    and chopped, + 2 Tbsp
    slices for garnish

½ cup shredded mozzarella
    cheese

3 fat sausages

2 Tbsp almonds

You can make your own pie crust, but for something like a quiche save time by purchasing a frozen one. Serve with crusty bread and deep regrets that you let Weyland-Yutani talk you into this mission.

1) Blind bake the crust at 375°F for 15 minutes. While it bakes, put a skillet over medium-high heat. Add the olive oil, onion, garlic, and chopped asparagus. Cook for 3 minutes, stirring often. Add the spinach one handful at a time, stirring well, until it's all wilted. Add the basil leaves and continue stirring for 1 minute, or until they're also wilted. Remove the pan from the heat.

2) In a bowl, beat the eggs, cream, salt, and pepper together.

3) Remove the crust from the oven and spread the cheddar across the bottom. Sprinkle the chopped roasted red bell peppers and the rest of the vegetables into the crust, then pour the egg mix into the crust to cover the fillings.

4) Bake at 350°F for 30 minutes. Sprinkle the mozzarella cheese on top and continue baking for another 15–20 minutes.

5) While the quiche bakes, poke the sausages a couple of times with a fork. Pop them in the oven so the skins will crisp up nicely. They should be ready when the quiche is done.

6) Once the sausages and quiche are done, remove them from the oven and push a line of slivered almonds into one end of one sausage to create a mouth. Cut the other end of the sausage on a diagonal, making a flat surface. Poke it into the middle of the quiche. Arrange some extra strips of roasted red bell pepper around the base where it emerges.

7) Meanwhile, cut the other 2 sausages into coins. Arrange those around the base of the quiche to give it more of a 3D meaty explosion effect.

FRENCH ROLLED OMELET
WITH HERBS AND PEPPERS
MAKES TWO SERVINGS

This will make two omelets. Ideally, you'll be able to link them together to make one chestburster big enough to feed (on) a crew of four. French omelets require a deceptive amount of skill to make – don't worry if your first attempts look more like the chest than the burster.

1) Place an 8-inch skillet over medium heat. Let the pan warm up while you beat the eggs, milk, kosher salt, and fresh ground black pepper until it's a slurry.

2) Melt 1 Tbsp butter at the bottom of the pan. Pour half the egg mix into the pan and tilt it gently so the pan is evenly coated. Use chopsticks or a spatula to gently stir the eggs for the first 2–3 minutes, until small curds form. Jostle the pan to settle the egg mix over the entire base of the pan. Turn the heat down to low.

3) Sprinkle half the herbs onto the omelet. Top with half the grated Parmesan cheese.

4) Once the surface of the eggs is wet, but no longer runny, use a rubber spatula or chopsticks to gently roll the omelet up from one side to the other so it forms a pallid, phallic tube. Slide it onto a plate, cover, and repeat the process for the second omelet. If possible, try to make one end thicker than the other. The thinner end will be the chestburster's tail.

5) Add 1 tsp olive oil to a pan and sear the onion strips, stirring often until they're just past translucent and starting to brown at the edges.

6) To assemble the breakfast of horrors, remove the tomato stem and arrange your omelets so that one of them seems to be sticking straight up and resting its evil little head on the tomato. Nestle the fatter end of the second omelet against the end of the first to give the illusion of one continuous tube and let the second omelet drag out to the other side of the plate. If one end is thinner, try to curl it like a tail.

7) To make the face, cut the onion strips so they fit into the 'mouth' region of the omelet. Use a sharp knife to score the onion so it looks like teeth. About 1 inch back from the mouth, press thinly sliced roasted red bell pepper strips into both sides of the omelet, kind of like racing stripes. Use the dull side of a butter knife to gently press in and score the 'tail' omelet to create a segmented tail.

8) To complete the freshly erupted look, carefully spoon romesco sauce around the omelets. You can use the sauce to help hide any seams. Arrange the rest of the onion slices on the plate so they look like the damaged guts the chestburster is emerging through.

PREP: 20 MINUTES
COOK: 5 MINUTES

 DIETARY: V, GF, KE*, KD, H

 METHOD: EASY

INGREDIENTS

5 large eggs

¼ cup heavy cream
or whole milk

½ tsp kosher salt

¼ tsp freshly ground
black pepper

2 Tbsp unsalted butter

3 Tbsp finely chopped fresh
herbs, such as chives,
thyme, or basil

4 Tbsp grated Parmesan
cheese

1 tsp olive oil

¼ white onion, cut into
½ inch x 2 inch strips

1 large tomato (optional)

2 Tbsp roasted red
bell pepper strips

1 cup romesco sauce
(see page 130)

CHESTBURSTERS

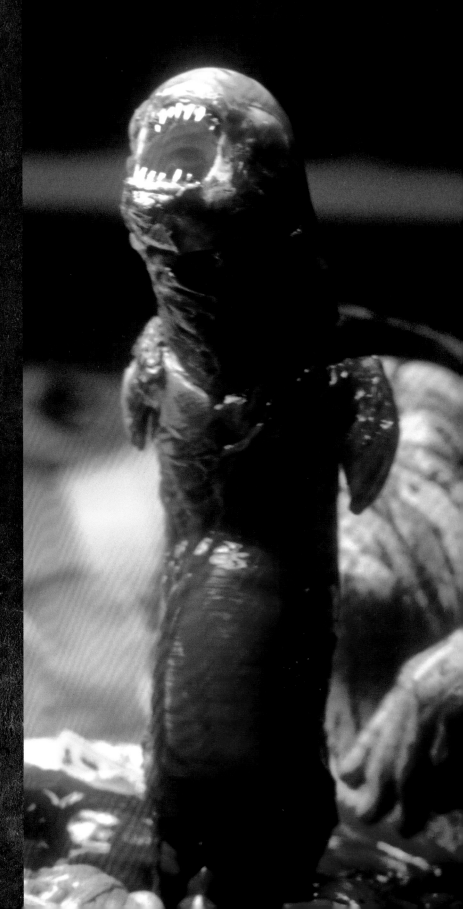

COILED CHESTBURSTER VEGGIE PASTILLA

MAKES SIX SERVINGS

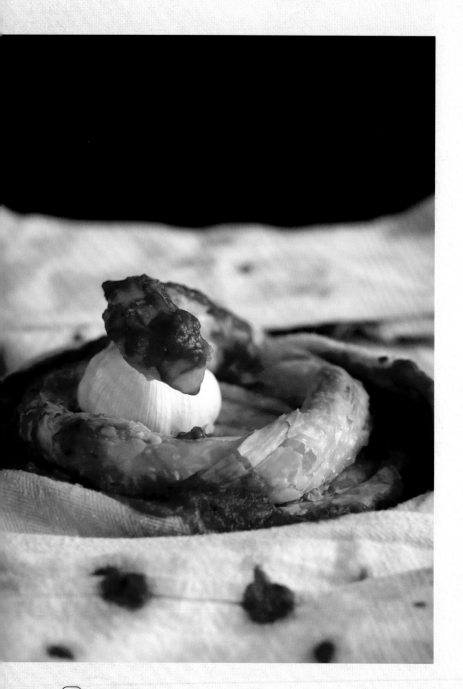

INGREDIENTS

2 Tbsp olive oil, divided

1 Tbsp cinnamon

1 tsp ground cumin

½ tsp ground coriander

½ tsp salt

1 ½ lbs sweet potatoes

1 10-oz bag spinach

6 garlic cloves, crushed and chopped

½ yellow onion, peeled and sliced thin

1 box frozen filo pastry, thawed

16 oz jar red bell peppers, drained and cut into thin strips

16 oz feta cheese

1 stick butter, melted

2 Tbsp red pepper flakes (optional)

1 tiny radish (optional)

1 cup romesco sauce (see page 130)

1) Preheat the oven to 400°F. Peel the sweet potatoes and cut them into 2-inch cubes.

2) Pour 1 Tbsp olive oil into a large mixing bowl. Mix in the cinnamon, cumin, coriander, and salt. Toss the potato chunks in the oily spice blend until they're well coated. Arrange them on a baking sheet in a single layer and bake for 30 minutes, or until the sweet potatoes are cooked through and soft. Remove from the oven and cool.

3) While the sweet potatoes cook, wilt the spinach. Add 1 Tbsp olive oil to a large skillet over medium-high heat. Add the spinach a handful at a time, stirring constantly. When about half of the spinach is wilted, toss in the garlic and onion. Keep stirring, cooking for another 2–3 minutes until all the spinach is wilted, the garlic is lightly browned, and the onions are translucent. Tip it all into a bowl and set it aside to cool.

4) When everything is cool enough to touch, lay out a 3-foot long piece of parchment paper. Lay three sheets of filo stacked on the parchment paper. Lay three more at the end of that so the bottom 2 inches overlap. Lay 3 more at the end of that one, also overlapping by 2 inches. With a pastry brush, coat the whole mess generously with butter. Paint on a little extra around the seams. Repeat with stacks of three, painting each with butter, until you end up with a rectangle that's nine sheets tall. Reserve any extra filo to patch any holes.

5) Grab the potatoes and mash them gently with a fork. Arrange the sweet potatoes in a 4-inch thick line, about 3 inches from the edge of the filo rectangle, stretching the whole length of the rectangle. Top that with the roasted red pepper strips, then with the spinach/onion/garlic mix. Finish it off with feta.

6) Starting at the edge closest to you, lift the filo and fold it over the filling. Roll it up, aiming away from you, until it looks like a long white sausage. Don't worry if it splits. Butter any holes, and patch them with some spare filo. Once the pastry is rolled into a tube, gently coil it up into a circle. Tuck both ends underneath the coil.

7) Paint the whole thing with butter or oil then gently sprinkle with the red pepper flakes. Rip off the excess parchment paper. Use what's left to carefully lift the pastry onto a baking sheet.

8) Bake for 45–50 minutes, or until a crispy golden-brown. Let it rest for at least 10 minutes before serving. Just before serving, cut a ¼ inch slice of onion a little wider than the coil. Score it with a knife to make teeth. Cut off the outer end of the pastry coil and tuck the 'teeth' into the filling. If you'd like it on a bloody bedding for presentation purposes, try drizzling the romesco sauce into the seams of the spiral.

CHESTBURSTER STROMBOLI

 PREP: 10 MINUTES
COOK: 15 MINUTES

 DIETARY: V*, KD*, H

 METHOD: EASY

INGREDIENTS

One ball of purchased,
   refrigerated pizza dough

1 Tbsp cornmeal

1 Tbsp olive oil

1 cup marinara sauce

1 cup pepperoni slices

1 cup cooked sausage crumbles

½ cup yellow onion,
   peeled and diced

½ cup green peppers,
   seeded and diced

1 cup mozzarella cheese,
   shredded

½ cup + 2 Tbsp Parmesan
   cheese, shredded
   and divided

1 tsp oregano

½ tsp onion powder

¼ tsp garlic powder

1 egg, lightly beaten

Extra marinara sauce
   for dipping

1) Preheat the oven to 475°F. Roll out a sheet of parchment paper and lightly dust with cornmeal. Roll the pizza dough ball into an 8 x 16-inch rectangle.

2) Spread the marinara sauce over the dough, leaving a solid 2-inch margin all around the crust. Top with the pepperoni, sausage, onions and peppers. Spread the mozzarella and ½ cup Parmesan over the meats and veggies. Finish it off by sprinkling on the oregano, onion, and garlic powders.

3) It's time to roll this monster up into a chestburster. Start with the edge closest to you and carefully roll away as tightly as possible. Use the parchment paper to help guide the dough and hold it in place. Pinch the seam closed and roll the stromboli seam side down. Carefully pinch the ends closed so it's nice and seamless and tuck it as far under the stromboli as possible. Let the dough rest for 3–4 minutes. It's been through a lot.

4) Use the parchment paper to lift the dough onto a baking sheet or pizza stone. Turn over a ramekin and carefully slide it between the parchment paper and the baking sheet, beneath the 'head'. You want your stromboli to rise up like a cobra. Arc about half of the body upward, then wiggle the back end so it looks like it's in motion.

5) When you're happy with the tail end, press the back of a butter knife into the front of the chestburster's face to make a line for the mouth. Don't pierce the dough; just push in enough that there's a clear, wraparound mouth.

6) Use a pastry brush to paint your chestburster with the beaten egg. Sprinkle the surface with the remaining Parmesan cheese. Use a sharp knife to score the wiggly back end every 2 inches. This allows steam to escape and gives the chestburster's body familiar ridges.

7) Bake for 10–12 minutes, until the top is golden-brown, and the cheese tries to bubble through the slits. Let it rest out of the oven for at least 5 minutes before messing with it. Transfer the stromboli to your serving platter. Fill the ramekin with extra marinara and prop it under the chestburster's chin. Spread a bit of marinara on the platter so it looks like the chestburster is dragging a trail of blood behind it.

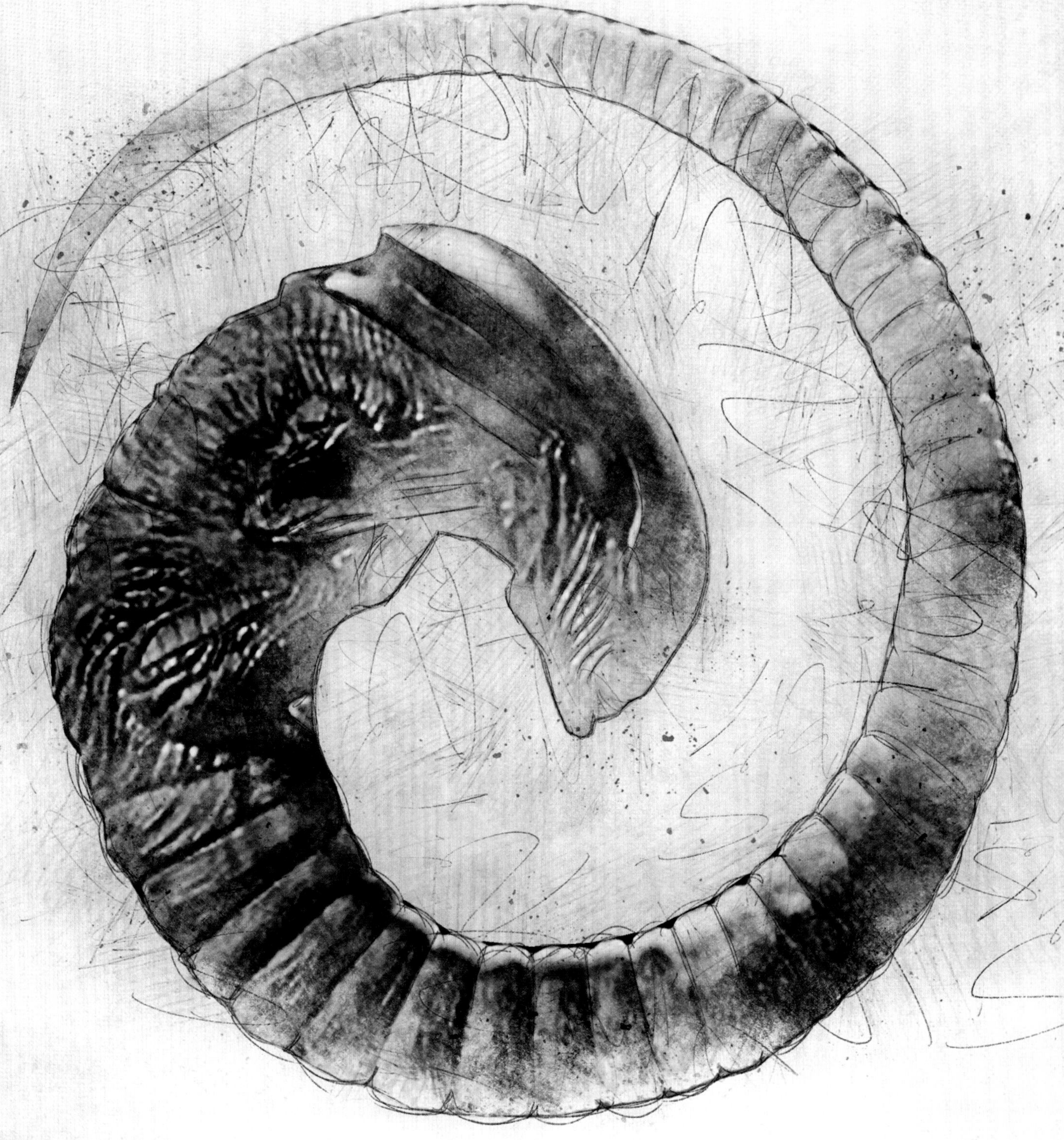

ZUCCHINI AND YELLOW SQUASH GRATIN

MAKES FOUR TO SIX SERVINGS

PREP: 15 MINUTES
COOK: 40 MINUTES

DIETARY: V, GF, KE, KD, H

METHOD: EASY

INGREDIENTS

3 zucchinis

2 yellow squash

¼ cup salted butter

1 small yellow onion,
thinly sliced

6 garlic cloves, minced

8–10 fresh basil leaves

¾ cup heavy cream

½ tsp fresh ground
black pepper

½ cup shredded
Parmesan cheese

2 cups shredded
Gouda cheese

1 cup shredded
mozzarella cheese

1 Tbsp slivered almonds

1 8-oz can basil and garlic
tomato sauce (optional)

1) Cut the yellow squash and two of the zucchinis into ¼ inch rounds. Arrange the rounds in a circular pattern in a pie pan, so each piece overlaps the other. Set aside.

2) Preheat the oven to 450°F.

3) Melt 2 Tbsp butter in a large skillet over medium heat. Add the onion and cook 5–7 minutes, stirring occasionally. Add the garlic and cook for another 1–2 minutes, or until the garlic starts to barely brown. Add the basil leaves and stir for 1 minute, letting them wilt slightly.

4) Melt the rest of the butter. When it's frothy, pour in the cream and simmer until bubbly. Add the black pepper and Parmesan. Continue stirring until the cheese is fully melted.

5) Pour the cream mix over the sliced zucchinis and squash. Top with the shredded Gouda.

6) Bake for 20 minutes, or until the cheese is bubbly and golden brown. Top that with the mozzarella shreds, turn the heat down to 400°F, and put the gratin back in the oven for another 5 minutes, or until the cheese is melted and the surface is nice and white.

7) While the gratin bakes, peel the remaining zucchini. Cut off the stalk end on a slight diagonal so the zucchini will stick up when you shove the chestburster into the middle of the gratin. Cut a shallow 'racing stripe' along the sides of the head and cut a shallow line in front for the mouth. Shove slivered almonds into the mouth to create pointy teeth.

8) When the gratin comes out of the oven, shove the flat end of the chestburster zucchini right into the middle so it pokes up as if emerging from a body. If you'd like, spoon a little herbed tomato sauce around the exit wound so it looks more like your chestburster just shot up through a plain white t-shirt.

CUCUMBER CHESTBURSTER SHAVED SALAD

MAKES FOUR TO SIX SERVINGS

 PREP: 5 MINUTES

 DIETARY: VE, V, P, GF, KP

 METHOD: EASY

This all-white vegetable salad gives the effect of a rumpled company issue t-shirt with a baby chestburster poking through. If you're confident using a mandolin, this comes together in five minutes; if you don't have a mandolin, use a knife and some patience to cut everything very thin.

1) Peel one cucumber, the jicama, and the green apple. Cut the base off the fennel. Run everything through the thinnest blade on your mandolin so the slices are all equal thickness (or cut them as thinly as possible with a sharp knife). Toss the veggies in a large bowl, then scatter them across your serving dish.

2) Peel the second cucumber. Cut a shallow line around the 'head' to create a mouth and carve racing stripes. Jam slivered almonds into the 'mouth' to make teeth.

3) To make the vinaigrette, whisk all the ingredients together in a jug until combined.

4) Place the carved cucumber into the salad so it looks like it's just emerging. Drizzle salad dressing around the base of the cucumber, and artfully splash a little more around so it looks like blood droplets. Set the rest of the dressing aside for people to add to their individual portions.

INGREDIENTS

SALAD:

2 large cucumbers

3 medium radishes

1 jicama

1 bulb fennel

1 green apple

1 Tbsp slivered almonds

VINAIGRETTE:

⅓ cup olive oil

⅓ cup pomegranate juice

¼ cup red wine vinegar

2 Tbsp maple syrup

2 tsp Dijon mustard

⅛ tsp fresh cracked
   black pepper

ERUPTING MANICOTTI IN FETTUCCINE ALFREDO

MAKES FOUR TO SIX SERVINGS

Not gonna lie. This recipe is a bit fussy. You only need 12 manicotti noodles, but boil 16 because some of them are going to rip and you'll want spares.

MANICOTTI

1) Boil the manicotti noodles according to package directions. Preheat the oven to 350°F.

2. While the noodles boil, put a large skillet over medium heat. Add 1 Tbsp olive oil. Cook the onions for 4–5 minutes, or until translucent. Add the garlic cloves and cook for another minute. Start adding the baby spinach one handful at a time as it wilts down. Repeat until all the spinach is wilted. Remove from heat. Mix in the ricotta, cream cheese, 1 cup mozzarella, ½ cup Parmesan, Italian seasoning, and fresh ground black pepper. Beat until smooth.

3) Once the manicotti noodles are cooked, drain them and carefully spoon in the spinach and cheese mix. Pack it in as tight as you can without bursting them, but don't push it all the way to the ends. Fold

the pointy end down and tuck it into the open end of the noodle to seal the noodle shut. Hold the seal in place with toothpicks. Repeat for the other end. Repeat until you've successfully stuffed and sealed at least 12 of the noodles.

4) Pour half the pasta sauce into a greased baking tray. Neatly arrange the manicotti in a single layer and pour the rest of the pasta sauce on top. Cover with foil.

5) Bake for 25 minutes. Remove the foil and sprinkle the mozzarella and Parmesan. Bake for another 5–10 minutes, or until the cheese is melted.

FETTUCCINE

1) Boil the noodles according to package directions and drain. Save ½ cup of the pasta water.

2) Put a saucepan over medium heat. Melt the butter until its frothy. Pour in the cream, salt, and pepper. Sprinkle in half the Parmesan and keep stirring until the cheese melts. Add in half of the remaining Parmesan. Once more, keep stirring until it melts.

3) Add in the fully cooked fettuccine noodles and stir well. When the noodles are thoroughly coated, sprinkle in the last ¼ cup of Parmesan cheese. Stir well. If the sauce is too thick, try adding 1 Tbsp pasta water at a time to thin it to your desired consistency.

FINISHING

1) For each plate, place four 3-inch wedges of garlic bread to prop up the chestbursters so it looks like they're peeking up out of a body. Arrange the fettuccine alfredo around the garlic bread. The noodles are your innocent victim's intestines. Lay one manicotti on each wedge of garlic bread. Layer another one behind it, to create a tail. Arrange a little fettuccine over the seams where the two manicotti join up. Xenomorphs are wily and will slip in and out of a person's guts. Score an onion slice and tuck it into the bottom of the manicotti faces so it looks like sharp little teeth. Carefully remove all the toothpicks before serving. If you only need one presentation plate, then let people admire your Xenomorph craftsmanship while serving

PREP: 20 MINUTES
COOK: 1 HOUR

DIETARY: V*, KD, H

METHOD: MODERATE

INGREDIENTS

16 manicotti noodles

1 Tbsp olive oil

1 medium yellow onion, peeled and diced
(reserve 12 slices for teeth)

6 garlic cloves, minced

10 oz baby spinach

3 cups ricotta cheese

8 oz cream cheese, softened

2 cups mozzarella cheese, divided

¾ cup grated Parmesan cheese

1 Tbsp Italian seasoning

1 tsp fresh ground black pepper

3½ cups marinara sauce
(see page 129), or 26-oz jar marinara

Toothpicks

1 lb fettuccine noodles

1 stick butter

¾ cup heavy cream

1 tsp salt

1 Tbsp fresh ground pepper

2 cups grated Parmesan cheese

Purchased garlic bread, baked

WHOLE ROASTED CARROT CHESTBURSTER SURPRISE

MAKES FOUR TO SIX SERVINGS

 PREP: 15 MINUTES
COOK: 35 MINUTES

 DIETARY: VE, V, P, GF, KP, H

 METHOD: EASY

INGREDIENTS

2 lbs (about 12) long,
    fat white and
    yellow carrots

2 Tbsp olive oil

1 tsp sweet paprika

1 tsp garlic powder

½ tsp onion powder

1 tsp cumin powder

½ tsp coriander powder

1 tsp salt

½ tsp fresh ground
    black pepper

DRESSING:

2 Tbsp honey

2 Tbsp lemon juice

1 tsp ginger paste

½ tsp kosher salt

1) Preheat the oven to 400°F. Spread parchment paper over a baking sheet.

2) Peel the carrots and cut off the stem end. Use a paring knife to round the cut end out. It's going to be the chestburster's face. If you have a mandolin, cut two long strips off the bottom of the carrots to keep them from rolling.

3) The pointy end of the carrots will be the chestbursters' tails. To create the ridged tail effect, use the paring knife to cut shallow grooves every inch or so up the length of the carrot until you reach the 'head' area. Leave that smooth. Cut a line into the front for the 'mouth'. Repeat for all the carrots.

4) Mix the olive oil and, paprika, garlic, onion, cumin, coriander, salt, and pepper. Smear it over the carrots until they're thoroughly coated.

5) Arrange the carrots in a single layer on the parchment-lined baking sheet. Make sure the cut side is facing up and the smooth side facing down. Bake for 30–35 minutes. The carrots should be soft all the way through and able to bend without breaking.

6) Mix the honey, lemon juice, ginger paste, and salt. Drizzle over your freshly baked chestbursters to give them a wet, organic look (and a nice flavor). You can serve these immediately or store them in the fridge to pop out of meals for the next 4–5 days. You can create teeth by either scoring a bit of onion and shoving it in the mouth area or jamming in some slivered almonds.

THESE LITTLE GUYS EXIST TO ADD A BIT OF EXISTENTIAL HORROR TO ANY MEAL. LET THEM PEEK OUT WHEREVER IT AMUSES YOU TO HIDE THEM.

TURKEY TENDERLOIN CHESTBURSTER

IN PAPPARDELLE MARINARA

MAKES FOUR TO SIX SERVINGS

1) Preheat oven to 400°F.

2) Heat I Tbsp olive oil in a pan. Add the chopped mushrooms, crushed and chopped garlic cloves, and soy sauce. Cook for 3–4 minutes, or until the mushrooms are softened but not fully cooked through.

3) Add the spinach one handful at a time. Wilt it down, stir, and add more until the entire bag is wilted into the mix. Remove the veggie mix from the heat. Stir in the cream cheese, panko breadcrumbs, thyme, basil, salt and pepper. Set the filling aside.

4) Cut a deep slit down the side of the tenderloin and open into a butterfly, leaving at least a 1-inch deep join. Open it like a book then use a meat mallet (or your fist) to pound it down to ½-inch thickness. Spread the filling on the inside and roll the tenderloin up, jellyroll-style.

5) Use kitchen twine and start to truss the length of the tenderloin with butcher's knots. For the 'face' end, tie the string tight then leave about 3 inches of tenderloin before the next knot. After that, tie the knot tight and repeat every inch. This will help give the finished tenderloin the visual impact of a baby chestburster. If necessary, hold the bottom of the bare section closed with toothpicks.

6) Mix the Dijon mustard with 1 Tbsp olive oil, plus the garlic powder, onion powder, salt, and pepper. Coat the tenderloin with the mustard mix.

7) Tent foil over the top of the tenderloin and bake for 25 minutes. Remove the foil and bake for another 10, or until the interior temperature reaches 145°F and the juices run clear. Normally you'd want the tenderloin a nice golden brown, but for true authenticity you want it fully cooked but a little on the pallid side.

8) While the tenderloin bakes, boil the pasta according to package directions. When the pasta is fully cooked, rinse it under cold water to stop the cooking process and set it aside. Using the same pan, heat the marinara sauce over a low heat until warmed through.

9) Remove the tenderloin from the oven and cut away the twine. Prop the 'face' end of the tenderloin against the tomato so it looks like it's shooting straight up. Cut a line into the front and wedge the scored onion in to create a mouth. Optionally make shallow cuts along the sides and press in the roasted red pepper strips. Pile the pappardelle pasta over any cuts or joins, then loop it around on the plate like guts. The goal here is to make it look like the chestburster has punched through someone's small intestines. Spoon the marinara sauce over the pasta guts.

SERVE WITH GARLIC BREAD AND
ENJOY THE BODY HORROR!

**PREP: 30 MINUTES
COOK: 35 MINUTES**

DIETARY: N/A

METHOD: MODERATE

INGREDIENTS

2 Tbsp olive oil, divided

*½ lb mushrooms,
 roughly chopped*

*6 cloves garlic, crushed
 and roughly chopped*

½ Tbsp soy sauce

*10 oz bag baby spinach,
 chopped*

6 Tbsp full-fat cream cheese

½ cup panko breadcrumbs

*1 tsp fresh thyme leaves
 or ½ tsp dried*

*1 tsp fresh basil leaves
 or ½ tsp dried*

½ tsp salt

¼ tsp fresh ground pepper

1 ½–2 lbs turkey tenderloin

1 Tbsp Dijon mustard

1 tsp garlic powder

½ tsp onion powder

½ tsp fresh ground pepper

¼ tsp salt

8 oz pappardelle pasta

24-oz jar basil marinara Sauce

1 large tomato, stem removed

1 strip raw onion, scored

*2 long strips roasted
 red bell pepper (optional)*

SWEET AND SAVORY ROASTED SQUASH

MAKES FOUR SERVINGS

ORN SQUASH

Preheat the oven to 400°F. Cut the tops off the acorn squash and clean out the seeds and guts.

Mix the brown sugar, salt, and spice powder. Rub the interior of the hollowed squash with the sugar and spice mix. Mix the butter, honey or syrup and vanilla. Smear it over the interior of the squashes, on top of the spice blend.

Bake cut side up for 1 hour. The squash are done when the flesh is tender when poked with a fork.

LLOW SQUASH

Preheat the oven to 450°F. Set 2 of the yellow squash aside for final assembly. Meanwhile, cut the other two squash into 2-inch coins, then slice the coins in half.

Mix the olive oil, garlic, onion, salt, and pepper in a large bowl. Toss the squash pieces in the savory mix.

Put a piece of parchment paper on a baking sheet. Arrange the chopped squash in a single layer. Sprinkle 3 Tbsp of the grated

Parmesan on top. Bake for 20 minutes or until golden brown. Garnish with more cheese as soon as it comes out.

FINAL ASSEMBLY

1) Cut a slit in the end of the uncooked yellow squashes to form a mouth. Push in slivered almonds to make dangerous, pointy teeth. Use a paring knife to cut slits along the slides of the chestburster's head. Cut the base of the uncooked yellow squashes so that they'll stand up inside the baked acorn squashes.

2) Gently place a chestburster squash inside each of the baked acorn squashes. You might need a few toothpicks to hold them in place. Pour a little bloody salted caramel over the back half of the chestbursters so they look like they've popped out of a bloody wound. Feel free to drizzle more on the outside of the acorn squash for effect.

3) Pile the cooked savory yellow squash around the base of the acorn squash eggs. Complete the cute but creepy organic effect by garnishing with sprigs of fresh herbs.

INGREDIENTS

ACORN SQUASH:

2 acorn squash

¼ cup brown sugar, packed

1 tsp table salt

1 Tbsp pumpkin pie spice or Chinese five spice powder

¼ cup butter, softened

¼ cup honey or maple syrup

1 tsp vanilla

YELLOW SQUASH:

4 curved yellow squash, divided

2 tsp olive oil

1 tsp garlic powder

½ tsp onion powder

½ tsp fresh ground pepper

¼ tsp salt

¼ cup fresh grated Parmesan cheese, divided

FINISHING ELEMENTS:

¼ cup slivered almonds

1 cup bloody salted caramel (see page 127) (optional)

Sprigs of fresh thyme or rosemary

COILED APPLE STRUDEL
IN BLOODY SALTED CARAMEL SAUCE
MAKES FOUR TO SIX SERVINGS

Don't be ashamed to use a store-bought apple pie spice blend. Use 2½ tsp as a substitute for the individual spices. If you want, you can double the filling and save half as a topping for oatmeal or ice cream.

1) Preheat the oven to 375°F.

2) Core, peel, and chop the apples. Toss them in a saucepan along with the apple juice, brown sugar, cinnamon, allspice, ginger, nutmeg, and salt. Bring the whole mess to a boil then turn it down to low and simmer for about 15 minutes, or until the apples are tender. Let the filling cool completely.

3) Spread out a long piece of parchment paper. Unfold the puff pastry so the ends overlap by about 2 inches. Roll the pastry out until it's around 12 x 36 inches. Spoon the filling onto the conjoined puff pastry. Leave at least 2 inches bare around all the edges. Optionally drizzle ½ cup of bloody salted caramel over the apple filling.

4) Starting on the long side of the pastry sheet, roll it up, over the filling and away from you, as tight as you can. Use the parchment paper to help hold it in place as you roll. When you're done, gently pinch the seam closed. Tuck the ends underneath the pastry.

5) Coil the pastry. Pull the middle of the coil up and out so it lies over the inner coils. This will form the 'head' and make the final product look more like it's surging up from an open chest cavity. At the other end, pull the pastry out as long and thin as you can. Uncoil it a bit and give it a little wiggle, like the pastry is eager to escape once it knows the lay of your oven.

6) Leave the 'head' end of the pastry smooth but use the dull edge of a butter knife to press ridges in the hind end. Whisk an egg with 2 tsp of water and 1 tsp of vanilla extract. Use a pastry brush to paint the surface of the pastry. Bake for 25–30 minutes, or until golden brown.

7) When you take the pastry out of the oven, cut a line in the 'face' for the mouth. Poke two rows of slivered almonds into the 'mouth' area so the pointy teeth stick out. Drizzle the rest of the bloody salted caramel in the middle of the pastry, and a little into the seams where the coils touch.

PREP: 20 MINUTES
COOK: 45 MINUTES

DIETARY: VE*, V, KD, KP*, H

METHOD: EASY

INGREDIENTS

2 sheets puff pastry, thawed
  in a fridge overnight

4 medium apples

⅔ cups apple juice or
  non-alcoholic cider

¼ cup brown sugar

1 tsp cinnamon

½ tsp allspice

½ tsp ginger

¼ tsp nutmeg

⅛ tsp salt

1 large egg (omit vegan)

2 tsp water

1 tsp vanilla

2 cups bloody salted caramel
  (see page 127)

2 Tbsp slivered almonds

BANANA CREAM PIE TARTS

MAKES SIX TO EIGHT SERVINGS

 PREP: 1 HOUR 30 MINUTES
COOK: 30 MINUTES

 DIETARY: V, V, GF*, KD, H*

 METHOD: MODERATE

INGREDIENTS

CRUST:

¼ cup cold vodka

¼ cup cold water

2½ cups all-purpose flour

1 tsp salt

¾ cup cold, unsalted butter, grated or cut into small cubes

½ cup chilled solid vegetable shortening, cut into cubes

FILLING:

8 large egg yolks

½ cup cornstarch

6½ cups heavy cream, divided

3½ cups sugar

½ cup brown sugar

2 tsp vanilla

FINISHING:

1 cup heavy whipping cream, chilled

1 tsp vanilla extract

1 Tbsp powdered sugar

6 baby bananas

½ cup slivered almonds

1 cup bloody salted caramel (see page 127)

Remember, in order to simplify baking, you can always make the crust the night before. If you're rushed for time use a purchased, refrigerated pie crust.

CRUST

1) Mix the vodka and water. Put them in the fridge until they're nice and cold.

2) Whisk together the flour and salt. Use a pair of butter knives to mix the cold butter into the flour. When that's mostly combined, use the knives to mix in the vegetable shortening until the mixture resembles coarse crumbs. Sprinkle the cold vodka mixture over the top. Fold it into the crumbs until you achieve a tacky dough.

3) Divide the dough into two balls. Flatten the balls, wrap them in plastic, and chill them in the freezer for one hour or in the fridge overnight. You can leave it in the fridge for up to 2 days before using.

4) When you're ready to make your tarts, liberally butter a 12-hole muffin tin. Roll the pie crust out to ⅛ inch thickness. Cut the pie crust into squares large enough to have four flaps emerging from the tin and folded open on the pan itself. Gently push your square pie crust into the round holes. Arrange them so that the pie crusts don't touch each other.

5) Cover the muffin tin with plastic and pop it back in the fridge to rest for an hour. This will prevent shrinkage.

(continues over page)

6) After an hour, remove the plastic, poke fork holes at the bottom of each tart crust, and bake at 425°F for 15–20 minutes, or until both the top and bottom are golden brown. Check after 15 minutes and keep an eye on it after that. Once the tart crusts are nice and baked, set them aside.

FILLING

1) Whisk together the egg yolks, corn starch, and 2 cups of cream. Set aside.

2) In a large saucepan over medium heat, combine the rest of the cream with the sugar and brown sugar. Gently whisk it for 10 minutes as you bring it to a gentle boil. When the sugars are completely dissolved, turn the heat down to low. Scoop out 1 Tbsp of the cream and add it to the egg mix, whisking hard. This tempers the eggs so they don't curdle. Repeat this five more times, with six tablespoons of hot cream whisked into the egg mix one at a time.

3) Now we go in reverse: add ¼ cup of the egg mix to the cream, whisking constantly. Keep adding a little, whisking, adding a little more, and whisking,

until both mixes are fully incorporated. To ensure everything plays nicely together, keep whisking for another 5 minutes as the filling thickens.

4) Scrape all the filling into a glass bowl. Gently press plastic wrap right up on the surface of the filling so it doesn't form a skin and put it in the fridge for at least 2 hours, or until cool. When it's cool, scoop the pudding into your baked tart crusts.

FINISHING

1) Pour 1 cup chilled whipping cream, 1 tsp vanilla extract, and 1 Tbsp powdered sugar into a stand mixer and beat it on high until it turns into whipped cream. You can also beat it in a bowl with a hand mixer. Top the tarts with fresh whipped cream.

2) Now for the fun part! Cut your baby bananas in half. Use a chopstick to draw the 'racing stripe' line down each side of the head. Shove two lines of slivered almonds into the front to create a mouth. Repeat on all the bananas. Gently stuff one banana into each mini tart. For extra effect, you can optionally drizzle the tops with the bloody salted caramel.

TWICE-BAKED SWEET POTATOES
IN SALTED CARAMEL SAUCE

MAKES FOUR TO SIX SERVINGS

PREP: 10 MINUTES
COOK: 25 MINUTES

DIETARY: V, GF, KD, H

METHOD: EASY

INGREDIENTS

2 lbs Japanese white
  sweet potatoes

¼ cup butter

¼ cup milk

1 tsp ginger paste

¼ tsp salt

¼ cup + 1 Tbsp powdered
  sugar, divided

2 eggs yolks, divided

1 cup bloody salted
  caramel *(see page 127)*

1) Preheat your oven to 350°F.

2) Peel the sweet potatoes and put them into chunks. Place the chunks in a large, microwave safe bowl and fully cover them with water. Let them sit for 5 minutes.

3) Once they've sat, microwave the potato chunks in the water for 5–7 minutes, or until they're soft. Microwave temperatures may vary, so check the potatoes by pushing a fork into them. They're done when the fork penetrates with no resistance. Drain the sweet potatoes.

4) Add the butter, milk, ginger paste, and salt and mash them into the potatoes. Sprinkle in the powdered sugar and mix well. Keep sprinkling and mixing until you've incorporated all the powdered sugar. Beat in one egg yolk to help keep the mass together.

5) With damp hands, shape the sweet potato batter into a coil. The batter is very wet and will require a bit of attention and sculpting. Loop one end up so it seems to be peeking out of a cavity. Use the blunt end of a butter knife to score the body past the head area. Create a mouth by pressing the knife into the lower half of the face. Beat the remaining egg yolk with 1 Tbsp powdered sugar then use a pastry brush to paint it over the chestburster.

6) Bake for 15-18 minutes, or until cooked through and solid. Drizzle with bloody salted caramel to complete the just-punched-through-a-body effect.

BLOOD RED VELVET PIE

MAKES EIGHT TO TWELVE SERVINGS

INGREDIENTS

PIE:

1 frozen pie crust

4 large eggs + 1 egg yolk, divided

2 cups whipping cream, divided

⅓ cup cornstarch

½ cup sugar

⅓ cup unsweetened cocoa

1 cup buttermilk

2 Tbsp red food coloring

2 tsp vanilla extract

½ tsp almond extract

CREAM CHEESE TOPPING:

8 oz cream cheese, softened

¾ cup powdered sugar

¾ tsp vanilla extract

¼ tsp almond extract

⅛ tsp table salt

2½ cups heavy cream

FINISHING:

1 long iced donut
  (long john, iced finger,
  éclair, or similar)

2 Tbsp mini chocolate chips

If you can't find buttermilk, pour one cup of whole milk and remove 1 Tbsp. Add in 1 Tbsp lemon juice. Stir and set aside until it starts to curdle, about 5 minutes.

1) Blind bake the frozen pie crust according to packet directions. Set the pie crust aside to cool while you make the filling.

2) Beat the eggs, 1 cup of heavy cream, and the cornstarch together. Set aside.

3) Grab a large saucepan. Add the sugar and cocoa. Mix in the remaining cream and buttermilk. Bring to a boil over medium heat, whisking constantly. When the sugar is dissolved, turn the heat down to low.

4) Pour 1 Tbsp of the hot cream mix into the egg mix, whisking constantly. Keep adding 1 Tbsp of hot cream at a time, whisking constantly, until you've added 6 Tbsp. Now go in reverse; turn the heat on the saucepan back up to medium and pour in ¼ cup of egg mix, whisk it in thoroughly, and add another ¼ cup. Keep this up until all the egg mix is incorporated into the cream mix.

5) Keep whisking constantly until the mix thickens. Take it off the heat and whisk in the red food coloring, vanilla extract, and almond extract. Pour the mixture into your baked crust. Cover the top

with plastic and chill in the fridge for 4 hours, or overnight.

CREAM CHEESE TOPPING

1) Beat the cream cheese, powdered sugar, vanilla, almond extract, and salt at a medium speed until smooth and creamy. Pour in the heavy cream ½ cup at a time, beating between each mix. When all the cream is mixed in, keep mixing for another 2–3 minutes, until stiff peaks form.

FINISHING

1) Spread the cream cheese topping over the chilled pie.

2) Cut the bottom ⅓ off the donut. Poke two rows of mini chocolate chips into one end of the donut to create a mouth full of sharp little teeth. Shove the chestburster donut into the middle of the pie. Now pull it out. Shove it back in and out of the same hole a couple times so there's a little red peeking up through the top and it looks like the chestburster just punched its way out.

3) Optionally garnish with a few drops of red food coloring to give the top a lightly blood-spattered effect.

QUEENS

ALIEN QUEEN EMPANADAS

MAKES FOUR TO SIX SERVINGS

 PREP: 35 MINUTES
COOK: 30 MINUTES

METHOD: MODERATE

 **DIETARY: H***

INGREDIENTS

DOUGH:

4 cups all-purpose flour

2 tsp baking powder

2 tsp salt

1 stick (½ cup) cold butter, cut into cubes

1 cup cold water

1 tsp + 6 drops black food coloring, divided

1 egg (for final glaze)

FILLING:

1 Tbsp olive oil

1 yellow onion, peeled and diced (minus a few strips for the mouths)

2 jalapeños, minced, ribs and seeds removed

4 cloves garlic, minced

1 lb ground beef

1 lb ground chorizo sausage

15-oz can diced tomatoes

4-oz can mild green chilies

1 tsp chili powder

1 tsp smoked paprika

2 tsp cumin

1 tsp oregano

1 cup fresh cilantro leaves, chopped small

1 ¼ cup shredded Monterey Jack cheese

1 ¼ cup shredded cheddar cheese

24 small green onions (optional)

Easy restaurant-style salsa (see page 128)

DOUGH

1) Whisk together the flour, baking powder, and salt in a large bowl. Use your fingers to work the cold cubed butter into the mix until it resembles gravel. Mix 1 tsp of black food coloring into the cold water and pour the mix in, a tablespoon at a time, until it's integrated into the dough. Turn the dough out on a lightly floured surface and gently knead for 4–5 minutes. Put it back in the bowl, cover with plastic, and refrigerate for at least an hour.

FILLING

1) Put a large skillet over medium-high heat and add the olive oil. Cook the diced onions in the oil for 5 minutes, stirring often. Add the diced jalapeño and continue cooking for another 2–3 minutes. Add the garlic and continue cooking for an additional 2-3 minutes, or until it's soft and fragrant but not burned. Now add both the ground beef and the chorizo. Cook the meat until it's browned all the way through. Use a wooden spoon to break up clumps.

(continues over page)

2) Add the canned tomatoes, mild chilis, chili powder, paprika, cumin, and oregano to the skillet and mix well. Turn the heat down to medium and continue cooking for another 15 minutes. The mixture will reduce and thicken so it's less soupy. Remove it from the heat and scrape all the filling into a bowl to cool.

ASSEMBLY

1) Roll the dough out to ¼ inch thickness. Use a 4½-inch round cookie cutter to cut out rounds. Reroll the scraps to get more rounds.

2) Sprinkle a little Monterey Jack and a little cheddar in the middle of a round. Top with 1½–2 Tbsp of the meat filling. Fold the dough in half and crimp the edges.

3) Normally you'd make a half-moon shape with the seam pointing down, but we want these to look like Xenomorph Queens. Roll the crimped empanada so that the seam is on top. You want to make it into a sort of cigar shape with the crimped seam located ⅔ of the way down. The crimping forms the ridge that stretches back along the Xenomorph's head.

4) Give each cigar a gentle curve, then tug them a little so one end is wider than the other. The wider ends are the faces. Use the side of a spoon or the blunt side of a butter knife to press a mouth into each. Use a knife or a pair of kitchen shears to snip one into the shape of jagged teeth and press

the strips of reserved onion into the indentations you just made.

5) A finger's width back from the mouth, use a toothpick to press shallow lines into the bottom third of the head, all the way back to a finger's width from the end. Leave the top ⅔ nice and smooth.

6) Line a cookie sheet with foil and spritz it with nonstick spray. Arrange the heads on the foil, leaving 2 inches between them. Whisk the egg with 2½ tsp water and ½ tsp black food coloring. You can either paint the entire surface of the empanadas with egg wash or use a pastry brush to only paint the smooth top ⅔ in order to give them more of the movie's dual texture effect. Try it both ways to see which you prefer!

7) Preheat oven to 400°F. Bake the empanadas for 25–30 minutes. You won't be able to see that they're golden brown, but you can pick one up. If the back is soft, they're not done yet. If it's solid and crunchy, you're good to go.

8) To get the inner mouth effect, use a chopstick to make a hole in the very front of the mouth. Cut the roots off the white end of a small green onion and trim the white of the onion to round it out. Cut it about 3 inches from the end of the bulb. Gently slide the green end of the onion into the hole so it sticks out, creating the second chompy mouth of a Xenomorph Queen. Serve with easy restaurant-style salsa for human blood.

FROZEN CHOCOLATE-COATED BANANA QUEENS

MAKES TWELVE SERVINGS

 PREP: 10 MINUTES
COOK: 5 MINUTES

 DIETARY: V, GF, KD, H

 METHOD: EASY

INGREDIENTS

6 firm yellow bananas

12 popsicle sticks

1 Tbsp whole milk

1½ cups semi-sweet
chocolate chips

6 Tbsp dark chocolate
sprinkles

12 chocolat-dipped
cookie fingers

12 fresh raspberries

2 Tbsp whipped cream

White icing pen

1) Peel the bananas, cut them in half, and jam a popsicle stick in the cut end. Line a baking sheet with parchment paper.

2) Pour the milk over your semi-sweet chocolate chips. Microwave for 30 seconds. Stir, microwave again for 15 seconds. Keep microwaving for 15 seconds at a time, stirring between each microwave, until the chocolate is completely melted and smooth.

3) Dip the bananas in the melted chocolate one at a time. If the chocolate cools too much, microwave it for another 15 seconds and stir again.

4) To create the contrast between the top and bottom half of a Xenomorph queen's head, dip the top of her head into the dark chocolate sprinkles. Use a pastry brush to brush off any that get onto the bottom half.

5) Break off the chocolate end of each finger cookie and jam one in to each banana 'mouth', opposite from the popsicle stick end. Lay the chocolate coated bananas on the parchment paper-lined sheet and put them in the freezer until solid.

6) When they're solid, use the white icing pen to paint a mouth around the finger cookie. Add sharp, pointy teeth. To make the secondary mouth, stuff a raspberry with whipped cream and shove it on the end of the Pocky stick. Use a toothpick to draw lines in the whipped cream to represent teeth.

ROASTED PURPLE EGGPLANT ALIEN QUEEN HEADS

MAKES FOUR SERVINGS

 PREP: 15 MINUTES
COOK: 25 MINUTES

 DIETARY: VE, V, GF, P, KE, KP, H*

 METHOD: EASY

INGREDIENTS

2 large, dark purple, phallic shaped eggplants

2 Tbsp olive oil

1 Tbsp fresh rosemary

4 whole sprigs of rosemary

1 Tbsp fresh thyme leaves

4–6 fresh garlic cloves

¼ teaspoon kosher salt

⅛ teaspoon freshly ground black pepper

4 Tbsp slivered almonds

2 cups marinara sauce

Drizzle of balsamic vinaigrette

We're going to make a quartet of classic Alien Queen heads in profile.

1) Preheat your oven to 450°F.

2) Lay the eggplants on their sides. The widest part is the face while the narrow end with the stem is the long, trailing end of the head. Cut each down the middle, lengthwise, so each form two identical halves that can glare at one another.

3) Use a pastry brush to paint the eggplants with oil on all sides and put them cut side down on a lined baking sheet. Bake for 15–20 minutes, or until the eggplant has just started to shrivel at the edges.

4) While the eggplant bakes, mince the herbs and garlic and mix them together. Set the whole rosemary sprigs aside. Those are going to be your second mouths.

5) Pull the eggplants out of the oven and give them another quick touchup of fresh oil. Sprinkle the cut sides with salt and pepper, then smear with the garlic and herb mix.

6) Return them to the oven, cut side up, for 3–5 minutes. Remove the eggplants before the garlic burns and allow them to cool enough to handle.

7) Flip the eggplants skin side up. They'll be a bit wobbly, so use your fingers to gently smooth them into shape. Carefully cut a slit into the wide end to create a mouth. To fill it with teeth, carefully push slivered almonds into the top and bottom of the cut. Strip half the leaves off a sprig of rosemary and push the stripped end into the newly formed mouth so it pops out like a second mouth.

8) About two finger widths behind the mouth, cut a long, shallow slit lengthwise along the middle of the eggplant to help create the overall shape of the Alien Queen head. The eggplant's flesh will be soft, so press your thumb into it, just above the ridge you cut. Leave a thumb-width of space blank next to the first indentation, then press another indentation into it on the other side of the slit. Keep this up, pressing one space, leaving another blank, until you reach the end of the eggplant.

9) Arrange a circle of marinara sauce on a serving platter and lay your profile of an alien queen in the middle, drizzled with some acidic balsamic vinaigrette for the mingled human and Xenomorph blood.

ALIEN HAND ROLLS

MAKES FOUR TO SIX SERVINGS

 PREP: 20 MINUTES

 DIETARY: GF, KP, P*, KE*

 METHOD: EASY

INGREDIENTS

FOR THE SUSHI:

12 square sheets of nori

1 cup cooked sushi rice

½ cup julienned cucumbers

½ cup julienned carrots

½ cup julienned red or
    yellow bell peppers

12 small, round red radishes

1 bunch green onions

FOR THE TUNA:

¼ cup olive oil

2 Tbsp rice wine vinegar

1 Tbsp lemon juice

1 Tbsp lime juice

1 Tbsp freshly grated ginger

1 garlic clove, minced

2 tsp soy sauce

½ lb sushi-grade tuna steaks

1 Tbsp peanut or avocado oil

For this recipe we're following the template of the Xenomorph Queen started in the second movie and expanded on in the Aliens vs Predators franchise. Her very phallic head is replaced with a more insect-like, flared, triangular one.

SEARED TUNA

1) Pour the olive oil, rice wine vinegar, lemon juice, lime juice, grated ginger, minced garlic, and soy sauce into a zip-lock bag. Shake it until it's well mixed, then slip in the tuna steaks. Let them marinate in the fridge for 2–4 hours.

2) When you're ready to cook the tuna, put a skillet on high heat. Let the pan heat for 3–4 minutes. Add 1 Tbsp peanut or avocado oil. Using tongs, lay the tuna steaks in the pan. Sear for 1–2 minutes per side, depending on how well-done you like your tuna. Remove the tuna steaks from the pan. Squeeze half a lime over each cooked tuna steak and put them in the fridge to cool completely. You can do this up to one day in advance.

3) Before making your sushi, pull out the tuna steaks and cut them thinly against the grain.

ASSEMBLY

1) Put a square of nori in your hand. Spread 2 Tbsp of cooked sushi rice across the nori sheet. Top with a few strands each of cucumber, carrot, and bell pepper, then optionally 2–4 thin slices of seared tuna on top of that.

2) Normally at this stage you'd roll the sushi so it looks like an ice cream cone, but we're going to blunt the closed end so the 'mouth' isn't so pointy. Fold one corner of the nori sheet inward about an inch. Lay a thick strand of cucumber or carrot over the fold so it sticks out about 1½–2 inches. The veggie strand will become part of the queen's secondary mouth. Using the folded corner as the tip of the cone, roll the nori into a cone shape, taking care to make sure your 'tongue' sticks out.

3) To create the decorative carapace of an Alien Queen, cut a series of symmetrical holes in the nori toward the open end of the roll.

4) For each of the sushi rolls, take a radish and cut a smiling, toothy mouth into the pointed end to create the secondary mouth of the queen. Snip a section of green onion the length of the carrot strand emerging from the pointed tip of the sushi roll and thread the carrot strand through the green onion, then press the root end of the carved radish into the other end of the green onion. For presentation, make two rows of Alien Queen heads on a platter, so they appear to be facing each other and sticking out their tongues.

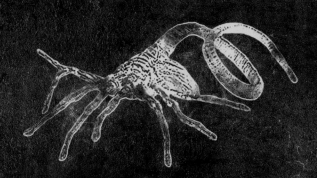

BAKED ACORN SQUASH SLIVER QUEENS

MAKES FOUR SERVINGS

RYE BREADCRUMBS

1) Cut 8 pieces of rye bread into cubes. Toss them with the garlic salt and onion powder. Spread them into a single layer on a parchment paper lined baking sheet. Bake at 400°F for 20–25 minutes or until crispy. Alternatively, leave the baking sheet out for 2–3 days, until the cubes are hard. Dump the dried or toasted bread cubes into a food processor and pulse until they become coarse breadcrumbs. Store any extra in an airtight container in a cool, dark place.

SQUASH

1) Preheat the oven to 400°F. Line a baking sheet with foil.

2) Cut the cap off the acorn squash. Scoop out all the seeds and guts. Cut the squash into segments, following the squash's natural seams. Each segment will end up a queen head.

3) In a separate bowl, mix the breadcrumbs, Parmesan, garlic, onion, salt, pepper, and minced thyme leaves.

4) If using, mix the black food coloring into the olive oil. Lightly drizzle the olive oil on the baking sheet and wipe the oil over the entire surface. Brush the individual slices of squash with oil.

5) Spread the breadcrumb mix on a plate and press the oiled squash slices into the mix. Carefully arrange the breadcrumb coated slices on the baking sheet. Lightly drizzle the squash with more oil.

6) Bake for 30–40 minutes, or until the squash slices are tender all the way through.

7) Snip off 3-inch pieces of rosemary. Strip the leaves off all but the top ½ inch to create the effect of a queen's inner mouth.

8) The wide end of each slice is the face. Cut a 1-inch slice into the bottom ⅓ of each queen's 'face' to create a mouth. Jam broken slivered almonds into the cut to create a mouth. Finish off the mouth by jamming the rosemary inside so it looks like the extra mouth is sticking out of the main one. Serve with bloody looking,

PREP: 30 MINUTES
COOK: 1 HOUR 5 MINUTES

DIETARY: V*, KO, H

METHOD: EASY

INGREDIENTS

SQUASH:

1 large acorn squash

¾ cup rye breadcrumbs

½ cup grated Parmesan cheese

1½ tsp garlic powder

½ tsp onion powder

¼ tsp salt

¼ tsp pepper

1 Tbsp fresh thyme leaves, minced

8–10 drops black food coloring (optional)

¼ cup olive oil

¼ cup slivered almonds

Orange-cranberry sauce (see page 131)

RYE BREADCRUMBS:

8 slices rye bread (or other black bread)

1 tsp garlic salt

1 tsp onion powder

BLACKENED CHICKEN WING QUEENS

MAKES FOUR SERVINGS

 PREP: 20 MINUTES
COOK: 1 HOUR 10 MINUTES

 DIETARY: GF, KE*, P*,
KD*, H*

 METHOD: EASY

INGREDIENTS

12 full chicken wings

¼ tsp black food coloring
(optional)

3 Tbsp olive oil

4 Tbsp blackening seasoning
(see page 126)

4 Tbsp shredded mozzarella
cheese (optional)

BBQ sauce of your choice

Chicken wings are normally cut into three pieces before being sold: the 'drumette', the part attached to the main body of the chicken itself; the 'flat' or 'wingette', the middle portion between the joints; and the 'tip', the pointy end piece. That's why your bucket of chicken wings often looks like it has bits from three different animals.

1) To create the effect you want, you need a full wing with all three parts. Use your hands to gently loosen them up. You don't want to break the joints entirely, but you do want to stretch them so that you can see all three distinct parts.

2) Preheat the oven to 375°F. Line a baking sheet with foil and spritz it with nonstick spray.

3) Mix the black food coloring into the olive oil. Use a pastry brush to liberally coat the wings with the black dyed oil. Put the blackening seasoning into a large bowl. Toss the oiled wings in the blackening seasoning.

4) Lay the wings out in a single layer on a baking sheet, leaving at least 2 inches of space between them. You may need two baking sheets. Don't overcrowd the wings. If you do, the skin won't get crispy.

5) Bake for 60–70 minutes, or until the skin is crispy and the meat has completely cooked through and has an internal temperature of 165°F.

6) If you'd like, create a mouth full of jagged white teeth by chopping the mozzarella shreds in half and arranging two lines of them, pointing at one another. Serve with a nice blood-red BBQ sauce.

PARMESAN ROASTED ZUCCHINI
WITH ACID NOODLES
MAKES FOUR TO SIX SERVINGS

PREP: 15 MINUTES
COOK: 20 MINUTES

DIETARY: V*, KE, KP, H

METHOD: EASY

INGREDIENTS

4 curved dark green zucchinis

½ cup freshly grated Parmesan

1 ½ tsp Italian seasoning

1 tsp kosher salt

½ tsp freshly ground pepper

4 Tbsp olive oil, divided

8 white onion strips

2 cups raw spiralized zucchini 'zoodles'

2 Tbsp freshly squeezed lemon juice

2 tsp lemon zest

2 Tbsp fresh basil, chiffonade

When picking out your zucchini, look for long ones that have a natural curve, preferably bulbous at the end and narrower near the stem. The key to making your zucchini nice and crispy instead of gross and squishy is to put a wire rack over your baking sheet. This lets the hot air circulate and prevents the zucchini from pooling in its own juices.

1) Cut the stem end off each zucchini at an angle, facing downward. Cut both zucchinis in half, lengthwise.

2) Preheat your oven to 400°F. Line a baking sheet with foil and put a wire rack on top of it.

3) Mix the Parmesan, Italian seasoning, kosher salt, and pepper. Rub the zucchini halves with oil. Toss them in the seasoned Parmesan so it coats all sides.

4) Spritz the wire rack with nonstick coating. Place the zucchinis cut side down on the rack with at least 2 inches of space between each one. If you crowd them, they'll get mushy.

5) Bake for 12–15 minutes. Without opening the oven, switch it to broil. Watch carefully for the next 2–3 minutes. You want the cheese to get crispy but not to burn. The moment you look away it'll turn on you. When it's perfect, turn off the oven and remove the baked zucchini halves.

6) Cut a mouth shaped hole in the bell end of each zucchini. Use a sharp knife to create jagged 'teeth' with strips of onion then shove it into the mouths.

7) Toss the raw zucchini noodles with lemon juice, lemon zest, fresh basil, and 2 Tbsp olive oil. Arrange the Queens so it looks like they're spewing white acidic zucchini 'blood.'

STUFFED POBLANO PEPPER QUEEN HEADS

MAKES SIX SERVINGS

PREP: 20 MINUTES
STEAM: 20 MINUTES
COOK: 20 MINUTES

DIETARY: GF

METHOD: MODERATE

INGREDIENTS

6 large, dark poblano peppers

2 tsp vegetable oil

1 lb raw chorizo sausage
(not in casings)

1 small red onion, minced

2 tsp dried oregano

1 tsp of cumin

½ tsp coriander

1 tsp table salt

½ tsp black pepper

15 oz can black beans,
drained and rinsed

6 cloves garlic, minced

4 Tbsp tomato paste

1 cup cooked rice

1 cup canned corn,
drained and rinsed

1 medium Roma tomato, diced

⅓ cup sour cream

⅓ cup fresh cilantro, finely
chopped, plus extra to garnish

1–4 tsp hot sauce, to taste
(optional)

6 Tbsp cotija cheese, grated,
plus extra for topping

¾ cups shredded Cheddar
Jack cheese

6 small dried chili peppers

6 pitted black olives

1) Preheat the broiler. While it's warming, line a baking sheet with foil and arrange the poblano peppers in a single layer, not touching. Broil them for 7–10 minutes, turning every 2 minutes so they char evenly. Once they've broiled and the skin has blackened in a few places, use tongs to transfer them to a glass bowl. Cover in plastic and let it sit for 20 minutes while the peppers hydrate and cool.

2) To make the filling, heat the oil in a large skillet over medium-high heat. Start by sautéing the chorizo until it's browned through. Add the onion and cook for another 3–4 minutes, stirring often. Add the oregano, cumin, coriander, salt, pepper, and the drained, rinsed can of black beans. Continue cooking for another 2–3 minutes, stirring often. Mix in the garlic and continue cooking for another 1–2 minutes. When it softens and becomes fragrant, stir in the tomato paste. Continue cooking for another 2 minutes, stirring often. Scoop everything into a large bowl.

3) Add the cooked rice, drained corn, diced tomato, sour cream, cilantro, hot sauce, cotija cheese, and Cheddar Jack cheese to the meat mixture. Mix well until evenly combined.

4) Remove the peppers from the bowl and carefully peel them. Cut the stem ends off. Use a spoon and a paring knife to remove as much of the seeds and stems as possible. Be gentle, as the peppers are fragile. Carefully spoon the filling inside, gently squeezing it down so the peppers are full but not at risk of bursting. Leave the last 2 inches of pepper unfilled.

5) Fold the unfilled pepper portion inward. This will create the 'face' and 'mouth' area of the queen. Use toothpicks to hold the pepper closed and the face in place. Use your hands to gently shape the peppers so they have the phallic yet tapered appearance of a Xenomorph queen. Put them back under the broiler for another 2–3 minutes, until they start to blacken.

6) Stuff the dried chili peppers into the pitted olives. This is now the creepy secondary mouth of your Xenomorph Queen. Cut a little slit into the front of the pepper and stuff the other end of the chili into the Queen's mouth so it sticks out like a hungry tongue.

7) Use a toothpick to very gently draw a line from the top of the mouth all the way back to the tail end of the head. Sprinkle a couple drops of hot sauce around the mouth as a finishing touch. Serve with smooth salsa and more cotija cheese.

HALF-HASSLEBACK BUTTERNUT SQUASH QUEEN

MAKES FOUR TO SIX SERVINGS

PREP: 20 MINUTES
COOK: 1 HOUR

DIETARY: V, VE*, GF, P, KD, H

METHOD: EASY

INGREDIENTS

2 curved butternut squashes

4 Tbsp olive oil

5 Tbsp blackening spice
(see page 126), divided

2 Tbsp melted butter

3 Tbsp maple syrup

1 tsp kosher salt

5–6 drops black food coloring
(optional)

4 Tbsp slivered almonds

1) Preheat the oven to 400°F.

2) Peel the exterior of the butternut squashes. Cut them in half lengthwise, then scoop out all the guts and seeds. Rub the top and bottom of the cut squash with olive oil.

3) Bake cut side down for 15–20 minutes, or until the flesh is soft enough to actually cut. Take it out of the oven and let it cool until you can touch it with bare hands.

4) Find a point ⅔ of the way down the wide, hollowed, bottom end of the peeled squash. This is the mouth end. Use a chopstick to draw a shallow but visible line from the front of the butternut squash to the back. For the first two inches of the line at the bell end, cut all the way through the squash. This will be the mouth.

5) Starting three inches behind the mouth slice the bottom ⅓ of the squash hassleback-style. Cut most but not all the way through the squash, spaced ⅛ inch apart. Stop slicing when there's still 3 inches

left at the very end. This creates the effect of the techno-organic ridges stretching the length of the Queen's head. Rub all four heads with a light coating of olive oil, then rub them all with the blackening seasoning until they're thoroughly coated.

6) Put the squash back in the oven and cook for another 20 minutes. While it bakes, mix the butter with the maple syrup, salt, and black food coloring.

7) When the squash has finished baking, remove from the oven and use a pastry brush to paint the top ⅔ of the heads with the maple mix. Leave the bottom ⅓ clear. This will give the top that shiny effect you see on top of an Alien Queen while leaving the bottom more matte. Bake for another 20–30 minutes, or until the flesh is cooked through at the widest part. Remove from the oven and allow to cool slightly.

8) When the squash cools enough to touch, jam the slivered almonds into the mouth to create sharp, angry teeth. If your top halves aren't shiny enough, carefully brush them with the remaining maple butter right before serving.

SWEET OR SAVORY ROAST PURPLE SWEET POTATO

MAKES FOUR TO SIX SERVINGS

 PREP: 20 MINUTES
COOK: 25 MINUTES

 METHOD: EASY

 DIETARY: VE, V, P*, GF, KP, H

INGREDIENTS

POTATO:

4–6 small, curved purple
   (Japanese) *sweet potatoes*

1 Tbsp olive oil

24 green onions with large,
   bulbous ends

SAVORY VERSION:

1 tsp table salt

1 tsp black pepper

1 tsp garlic powder

½ tsp paprika

SWEET VERSION:

1 tsp cinnamon

½ tsp table salt

¼ tsp nutmeg

¼ tsp allspice

⅓ cup cinnamon
   and cardamom balsamic
   reduction (see page 131)

These dark-fleshed tubers become even more menacing when roasted. Pick small sweet potatoes that are wide at one end and tapered at the other. The goal is to make these thick, with a lightly crispy exterior and a soft interior. The end result should look like classic Alien Queen heads in profile. This time, instead of them biting a marine's head off, you get to bite them first!

1) Preheat the oven to 400°F. While the oven preheats, peel the purple sweet potatoes. Decide which end is going to be the front and back, then cut each in half, lengthwise. Cut each piece in half again, lengthwise. You should now have two identical flat interior pieces and two more 3D curved outer pieces for each potato.

2) Mix up either the sweet or the savory spice mix by whisking all the ingredients together in a small bowl.

3) Coat the potatoes in olive oil, then coat in spice mix. Spritz a foil-lined baking sheet with nonstick spray and arrange the heads in a single layer, cut side down. Give them a little space to breathe.

4) Bake for 22–25 minutes. Test one near the middle. It should give easily when poked with a toothpick. Switch the oven to broil and put the potatoes back in for two minutes to get a truly crispy exterior.

(continues over page)

5) While the sweet potatoes bake, make garnishes from the green onions. They're destined to become the Xenomorph Queen's miniature interior mouth. Carefully cut away the roots while maintaining the spring onions rounded shape. Cut the onions down until they have about 2 inches of stem left. Save the green ends for another recipe. Cut a slit in the lower ⅔ of the bulb to create the mouth and use the tip of a sharp knife to make jagged marks simulating teeth.

6) When the potato slices are done, cut a 'mouth' in the lower ⅔ of the widest end of each potato. Use a chopstick to make a hole in the mouth and gently slide the green end of the onion into the hole so it sticks out, creating the second chompy mouth of a Xenomorph Queen.

7) Serve the savory fries with spicy ketchup and the sweet ones with cinnamon and cardamom balsamic reduction. If you work fast or just want to pretty a few up, dab your finger in the reduction and swipe a shiny line over the top half of each head, just above the mouth. That'll not only add a little flavor, but the contrast between the shiny and matte versions will imply more of the Xenomorph's distinctive head shape.

KOREAN-INSPIRED SALMON CEVICHE

MAKES FOUR SERVINGS

 PREP: 15 MINUTES
MARINATE: 4 HOURS

 DIETARY: GF, KE, P*, KD, H

 METHOD: EASY

INGREDIENTS

1 lb sashimi-grade salmon

14–16 limes

1 Tbsp gochujang

½ tsp sesame oil

½ tsp kosher salt

¼ tsp fresh ground
black pepper

2 cups cherry tomatoes

1 cup red onion

1 red bell pepper

Red food coloring (optional)

1 Tbsp olive oil

In honor of the Xenomorph's acidic spit and blood, here is a gory-looking recipe reminiscent of a fresh wound, entirely 'cooked' using acid instead of heat.

1) Chop the salmon into 1-inch cubes. Spread them in a single layer in a small dish and completely submerge them with lime juice. Start by juicing 10 limes. If you need more, add one at a time. Reserve 2–4 for a later step.

2) Cover the dish with plastic and put it in the fridge for around 4 hours to marinate. Less than that and the fish won't cook through. More and the acid will make the flesh start to fall apart in an unappetizing way. Stir once an hour to make sure all sides get evenly coated.

3) During the last hour, mix the juice of the remaining limes with the gochujang, sesame oil, kosher salt, and black pepper. Chop the tomatoes into chunks roughly the same size as the salmon and dice the onion and bell pepper. Mix the vegetables into the gochujang marinade and let them sit for an hour.

4) When the fish has marinated for four hours, drain the fluids. Scoop the fish out and add it to the gochujang and vegetable marinade. Give it all a good stir. If it's not red and wound-like enough, add red food coloring one drop at a time, stirring after each addition. When you're done, add in the olive oil and stir again.

5) Serve with shrimp or rice crackers.

OVEN ROASTED PEARS

WITH BALSAMIC AND HONEY

MAKES FOUR SERVINGS

PREP: 20 MINUTES
COOK: 30 MINUTES

 DIETARY: V, GF, P, KD, H

 METHOD: MODERATE

INGREDIENTS

4 firm Bosc pears

4 Tbsp butter

6 Tbsp raspberry
balsamic vinegar

4 Tbsp honey

3–4 fresh rosemary sprigs

4 Tbsp slivered almonds

½ tsp kosher salt

Red vanilla whipped cream
(see page 127)

1) Preheat your oven to 400°F

2) Don't peel the pears. Cut them in half, lengthwise, and core them. The bottom of the pear is going to be the mouth while the stem end will be the trailing head of the Alien Queen. Slice into the bottom of each pear a little to help create a mouth later on.

3) Use a small spoon to carve a groove from the stem-tip to the core. This is to help create the top and bottom effect of the queen's head. Designate a side as 'top'. From the core to the tip, score the 'bottom' using shallow, diagonal lines ⅛ inch apart to create the Queen's distinctive cranial texture. Cut a wedge from the center of the scooped-out core to the bottom of the pear to create a 'mouth'.

4) Put a Dutch oven on the stove over medium-high heat for 3–4 minutes so it can warm up. Melt the butter in the bottom of the pot. Lay the pears in a single layer, cut side down, and cook them for 2–3 minutes. Put the pot in the oven and cook the pears for another 20 minutes without touching them.

5) Remove the pot from the oven and drizzle the raspberry balsamic over the pears, then return them to the oven and continue cooking for another 5 minutes.

6) Remove the pot from the oven. Drizzle each pear with 1 tsp of honey and let them rest in the pot for 5 minutes. If you move them too soon, they'll fall apart.

7) Carefully remove the pears from the pot. Flip them over so the seared (cut) side is up. When they're cool enough to touch, wet your fingers and subtly shape the pears. Don't be afraid to squeeze them into submission slowly and surely so they don't suddenly break.

8) Jam slivered almonds into the 'mouth' to create sharp, pointy teeth. Cut 3-inch long segments of rosemary. Strip the leaves from the bottom 2 inches and jam the bare end into the Xenomorph's mouth to create the secondary mouth.

9) Spoon pan juices over the pears, then drizzle them with another 1–2 tsp of honey each. Finish with a scant sprinkle of kosher salt. Serve on a bed of red vanilla whipped cream so it looks like the Queens are resting in a pool of human blood and gore.

SAUCES

BLACKENING SEASONING

INGREDIENTS

4 Tbsp cayenne pepper
  (adjust to taste)

3 Tbsp smoked paprika

1 Tbsp sweet paprika

6 Tbsp garlic powder

3 Tbsp onion powder

1 Tbsp celery salt

3 tsp fresh ground
  black pepper

1 tsp white pepper

2 tsp dried oregano powder

2 tsp dried thyme powder

1 cinnamon stick

DIETARY: VE, V, GF, P, KE, KP, H

USED IN: Blackened Chicken Wing Alien Queen Heads, Half-Hasselback Butternut Squash Queen Heads

1) Mix everything in a small mason jar. Store it in a cool, dark place. Stir it with the cinnamon stick and shake it once a week. Leave the cinnamon stick in the jar when you scoop out spices. When it runs low, mix up more in the same jar, stir it with the cinnamon stick, and continue shaking once a week.

BODY-MELTING CITRUS SAUCE

INGREDIENTS

Juice of 2 limes
  (about 2 Tbsp)

Juice of 2 lemons
  (about 4 Tbsp)

2 cloves garlic

2 jalapeños, seeded

1–2 habanero peppers,
  seeded (optional)

1 tsp salt

¼ cup olive oil

DIETARY: VE, V, GF, P, KE, KP, H

USED IN: Roasted Whole Watermelon Radish Eggs in Body-Melting Citrus Sauce

1) Devein and deseed the jalapeños (and habaneros, if using). Be careful! The oils in the peppers will burn your eyes, nose, and nether regions if you touch them without washing all the acid off first! If in doubt, wear disposable gloves.

2) Toss the peppers and all the other ingredients into a blender or food processor and pulse it several times until the sauce is liquid. It'll be a little thinner and less oily than a traditional homemade vinaigrette. You can use this as a marinade for chicken or fish.

BLOODY SALTED CARAMEL

INGREDIENTS

4 Tbsp unsalted butter

1 cup packed light brown sugar

⅔ cup half-and-half

¼ tsp table salt

1 Tbsp vanilla extract

1 Tbsp red food coloring

1 Tbsp pink sea salt flakes

 DIETARY: V, GF, KD, H

USED IN: Sweet Facehugger Breadsticks, Sweet and Savory Whole Roasted Yellow Squash Chestburster Emerging from a Roasted Acorn Squash, Coiled Apple Strudel in Bloody Salted Caramel Sauce, Japanese Twice Baked White Sweet Potatoes in Salted Caramel Sauce, Individual Banana Cream Pie Tarts with Banana Chestbursters

1) Melt the butter in a saucepan over medium-low heat. When its frothy, add the light brown sugar, half-and-half, and table salt. Cook for 5–7 minutes, whisking constantly. It'll thicken considerably as it cooks. Pour in the vanilla and half the food coloring and keep whisking for another minute. If you're happy with the color, stop there. If not, keep adding food coloring. The final texture should be thick, but still pourable. Before serving, finish with a sprinkle of pink sea salt flakes.

RED VANILLA WHIPPED CREAM

INGREDIENTS

1 cup cold whipping cream

1 tsp red food coloring

2–3 drops blue food coloring

1 tsp vanilla extract

 DIETARY: VE, V, GF, KP

USED IN: Oven Roasted Pears with Balsamic Vinegar and Honey

1) Pour everything into a metal bowl and beat on high until it achieves firm peaks. If you're not happy with the color, adjust in the first minute or so of mixing, while the cream is still liquid.

2) To make red velvet vanilla whipped cream, add 2 tsp creme de cocoa.

EASY RESTAURANT-STYLE SALSA

INGREDIENTS

15-oz can diced tomatoes with herbs (such as basil and garlic)

15-oz can diced tomatoes with chilis

1 Tbsp olive oil

6 cloves garlic

½ red onion, roughly chopped

1 Tbsp oregano

½ Tbsp cumin

1 tsp smoked paprika

1 tsp cayenne pepper

½ tsp fresh ground black pepper

1 tsp hot sauce (to taste)

¼ cup cilantro (optional)

Juice of ½ lime

4–5 drops red food coloring (optional)

1–2 drops blue food coloring (optional)

DIETARY: VE, V, GF, KE, KP, H

1) Dump everything but the food coloring into a blender. Pulse until it's completely smooth. If the color isn't bloody enough, add a little bit of the red (with a drop of blue) food coloring and pulse again until you're happy with the color.

USED IN: Hash Brown Quiche Cup Xenomorph Eggs, Kale Crusted Baked Potato Xenomorph Egg with Cheese Straw Facehugger Fingers, Alien Queen Empanadas, Acidically Hot Stuffed Poblano Pepper Queen Heads

MARINARA SAUCE

INGREDIENTS

4 Tbsp olive oil, divided

1 large yellow onion, chopped fine

2 stalks celery, chopped fine

2 carrots, peeled and chopped fine

4 garlic cloves, minced

2 32-oz cans crushed tomatoes

2 bay leaves

½ tsp kosher salt

½ tsp freshly ground black pepper

1 Tbsp balsamic vinegar

DIETARY: VE, V, GF, KE, KP, H

1) Put a stockpot or Dutch oven over medium heat. Add 1 Tbsp of olive oil and the onions and sauté until translucent, stirring occasionally. Add 1 more Tbsp of oil, then the celery and carrots. Cook for about 10 minutes, or until soft. Add the garlic and continue cooking for another 2–3 minutes.

2) Pour in the canned tomatoes in all their juices. Add the rest of the olive oil, the bay leaves, and the salt and pepper. Turn the heat down to low and simmer, uncovered, for about an hour, stirring occasionally.

3) After an hour, remove and discard the bay leaf. Stir in the balsamic vinegar.

4) Let the sauce cool completely before storing. The chunky bits add to the overall gory effect, but if you'd like it smoother, pour the cooled sauce in a food processor and pulse until smooth. It can be made up to 2 days in advance.

USED IN: Facehugger Cheeseball on Pull-Apart Crust Body, Chestburster Stromboli, Turkey Tenderloin Chestburster in Papardelle Marinara, Chestburster Manicotti Erupting from Fettuccine Alfredo with Garlic Bread, Roasted Purple Eggplant Alien Queen Heads

ROMESCO SAUCE

INGREDIENTS

16-oz jar roasted red peppers, drained

¼ cup oil packed sun-dried tomatoes, drained

¼ cup tomato paste

½ cup roasted, salted almonds

4 garlic cloves, crushed

1 Tbsp sherry vinegar or red wine vinegar

2 tsp smoked paprika

½ tsp cayenne pepper

½ tsp freshly ground black pepper

¼ cup olive oil

½ tsp table salt, to taste

6–10 drops red food coloring (optional)

DIETARY: VE, V, GF, KE, KP, H

USED IN: French Rolled Omelet with Fresh Herbs and Roasted Peppers, Chestburster Coiled Veggie Pastilla

1) Fill your food processor with the red bell peppers, sundried tomatoes, tomato paste, almonds, garlic, vinegar, paprika, cayenne, and black pepper. Pulse several times to get everything nice and mixed up. Start slow while the nuts are chopped and then blend for longer as it becomes more liquid.

2) While the blender is on, drizzle in the olive oil 1 Tbsp at a time until you reach your desired texture. If you like it chunky you might only want 1 Tbsp, but if you like it creamier you can put in the entire quarter cup. Salt to taste.

3) If you want it to look more like the fleshy bits from the interior of a fresh wound, add a couple drops of red food coloring and pulse to mix it all in. Keep adding the drops 1–2 at a time and mixing them until you're satisfied with the gore level.

ORANGE-CRANBERRY SAUCE

INGREDIENTS

1½ cups fresh cranberries

¾ cup fresh squeezed orange juice

⅔ cup brown sugar

⅓ cup white sugar

2 Tbsp dark rum

1 tsp pumpkin pie spice

1 cinnamon stick

 DIETARY: VE, V, GF, KP

USED IN: Baked Acorn Squash Sliver Queen Heads

1) Dump everything in a small saucepan. Cook the sauce over medium-high heat for 15–20 minutes, stirring occasionally. As the sauce reduces the cranberries will pop like opening Xenomorph eggs.

2) Remove from heat. The sauce will be gorily chunky. If you'd like a smoother sauce, put half of it into a blender or food processor and pulse until smooth, then mix it back into the rest of the sauce. Either serve immediately or make it up to 3 days in advance.

CINNAMON AND CARDAMOM BALSAMIC REDUCTION

INGREDIENTS

2 cups balsamic vinegar

3 Tbsp brown sugar

1 cinnamon stick

1 cardamom pod

½ tsp vanilla extract (optional)

 DIETARY: VE, V, GF, KP

USED IN: Sweet or Savory Roasted Purple Sweet Potato Queen Heads

1) Pour the balsamic vinegar, brown sugar, cinnamon stick, and cardamom pod into a small saucepan and bring to a boil. Reduce the heat to medium low and simmer, stirring occasionally, until it's reduced down to ⅔ of a cup. It should take about 15–20 minutes. Don't try to rush it with more heat or you'll burn everything and it will make your house smell awful.

2) When the sauce is reduced add the vanilla, if you'd like. Pour everything into a mason jar and store it in a cool, dark place. Leave the cinnamon stick and cardamom pod in to give it extra flavor over time.

MEAL IDEAS

Whether you're planning a movie marathon, retro birthday, Halloween party, or even if you're just looking for a bold dinner party theme inspiration, these menu ideas should help inspire you to build a unique dining experience for your guests. Better to dine than be dined upon, after all…

ALIEN MARATHON VIEWING PARTY

Next time you host a viewing party, consider serving your guests (or victims) a selection of snacks that really draw them into the film. Serve with android-blood vanilla milkshakes.

Facehugger Cheeseball with Pull-apart Body
Alien Hand Rolls
Alien Queen Empanadas
Blackened Chicken Wing Queens
Frozen Chocolate-coated Banana Queens
Popcorn Ball Alien Eggs
Sweet Facehugger Breadsticks

SOPHISTICATED DINNER PARTY

Guide your guests through a sophisticated dégustation themed around the Xenomorph lifecycle. Serve with a dark red wine.

Stuffed Fig Xenomorph Eggs
Facehugger Cordon Bleu over Potato Skins
Zucchini and Yellow Squash Gratin
Oven-roasted Pears with Balsamic and Honey

ALIEN DAY BRUNCH

Celebrate Alien Day (April 26) with a delectable brunch to thrill and horrify your crewmates. Serve with Bloody Marys, for obvious reasons.

French Rolled Omelet with Herbs and Peppers
Red Pepper Quiche with Sausage Chestburster
Hash Brown Quiche Nests
Cucumber Chestburster Shaved Salad

HALLOWEEN HIGH TEA

Enjoy a classic English high tea with a terrifying twist on the creepiest day of the year. Serve with a choice of black coffee, loose-leaf green tea, or bitter gin and tonic.

Avocado and Bacon-stuffed Devilled Alien Tea Eggs
Pear and Cardamom Upside-Down Cake
Ginger, Avocado, and Coconut Mousse
Cheese-stuffed Mushroom Eggs

RETRO HORROR

Whether for a birthday, anniversary, or just because, commemorate the 70s through some truly horrifying flavors. Finish with a poisonously green Grasshopper, for added retro flair.

Retro Bologna Quiche Cups
Vintage Shrimp Facehugger
Banana Cream Pie Tarts

INDEX

DIETARY INFORMATION

This book does not represent dietary or religious advice. All dietary restriction labels are provided as a convenience. Please consult your own dietary guidelines or religious leaders for confirmation that recipes fit your needs. These designations are provided to help you include as many friends and family as possible at your Alien watch party.

Dietary restrictions are indicated throughout this book to make the recipes accessible to Alien fans of all dietary requirements. Use the key below to determine if a recipe fits your diet.

KEY	
SYMBOL	**DIET**
VE	Vegan
V	Vegetarian
GF	Gluten Free
P	Paleo
KE	Keto
KP	Kosher-Parve
KD	Kosher (contains meat or dairy)
H	Halal

Symbols with a '*' attached can be made to fit a dietary restriction with a small modification

Many spices are made in facilities that also process gluten. If preparing for someone who is gluten-free, only use spices are manufactured in a gluten-free facility. If cooking for someone who eats kosher or halal, source your meat from a certified kosher or halal supplier. If cooking for vegetarians or vegans, there is a wealth of tasty and convincing meat substitutes available now in most major supermarkets.

The following recipes can be lightly modified to fit specific dietary requirements:

RECIPE	DIET	MODIFICATION
AVOCADO XENOMORPH EGG	Paleo	Omit the tomatoes and sriracha.
ARTICHOKE & SPINACH DIP	Vegetarian	Use a vegetarian Parmesan style cheese.

RECIPE	DIET	MODIFICATION
SPICED ALIEN TEA EGGS	Keto, Paleo, Gluten Free	Use coconut aminos instead of soy sauce.
	Paleo	Omit brown sugar.
STUFFED GREEN PEPPER WITH GARLIC KALE	Keto	Use cauliflower rice or quinoa instead of rice.
POPCORN BALL ALIEN EGGS	Vegetarian	Use vegetarian marshmallows (without gelatin).
	Kosher-Parve	Use Kosher marshmallows (made with fish gelatin – not vegetarian).
OVEN-ROASTED BOK CHOY FACEHUGGERS	Paleo, Gluten Free	Use coconut aminos instead of soy sauce.
	All dietary restrictions	Omit fish sauce.
KALE-CRUSTED BAKED POTATO WITH CHEESY FINGERS	Kosher, Halal	Omit bacon.
INVASION OF POT PIES	Halal	Use broth instead of wine.
	Gluten Free	Omit the flour. Instead, mix 2 Tbsp corn starch with ½ cup of broth. Set aside until the carrots are cooked through. Pour it in slowly and mix so it thickens the broth. Use a gluten free pie crust.
SWEET FACEHUGGER BREADSTICKS	Vegan	Ensure the bread dough is vegan and the sugar has not been refined with bone char.
PEAR AND CARDAMOM UPSIDE DOWN CAKE	Halal	Use artificial vanilla and almond flavor instead of alcohol-based extracts.
COILED CHESTBURSTER VEGGIE PASTILLA	Vegan	Use olive oil instead of butter, and a vegan cheese substitute instead of cheese.
RED PEPPER QUICHE	Halal	Use halal-certified beef or chicken sausages
FRENCH ROLLED OMELET WITH HERBS AND PEPPERS	Keto	Omit tomato and peppers
CHESTBURSTER STROMBOLI	Vegetarian, Kosher-Dairy	Use vegetarian meat substitute.
	Halal	Use Halal pepperoni and sausage.
WHOLE ROASTED CARROT CHESTBURSTER SURPRISE	Vegan	Use maple or agave syrup instead of honey.

RECIPE	DIET	MODIFICATION
SWEET AND SAVORY ROASTED SQUASH	Vegan	Use vegan butter substitute instead of butter, and omit the Parmesan.
	Paleo	Omit the Parmesan.
	Vegetarian	Use a vegetarian Parmesan-style cheese instead of Parmesan.
COILED APPLE STRUDEL IN BLOODY SALTED CARAMEL SAUCE	Vegan	Omit egg, Serve without sauce or use a vegan caramel sauce.
	Kosher-Parve	Serve without sauce or use a vegan caramel sauce.
BANANA CREAM PIE TARTS	Gluten-Free	Use purchased, premade gluten free crusts
	Halal	Use an all-butter crust instead of a vodka crust.
FROZEN CHOCOLATE-COATED BANANA QUEENS	Gluten Free	Make sure to buy chocolate chips manufactured in a GF facility.
ROASTED PURPLE EGGPLANT ALIEN QUEEN HEADS	Halal	Omit balsamic vinaigrette.
ALIEN HAND ROLLS	Paleo, Keto	Use cauliflower rice instead of sushi rice, use coconut aminos instead of soy sauce.
	Gluten Free	Use coconut aminos instead of soy sauce.
BLACKENED CHICKEN WING QUEENS	Kosher	Omit mozzarella cheese.
	Paleo	Omit mozzarella cheese, use a paleo-friendly BBQ sauce, as most are not.
HALF-HASSLEBACK BUTTERNUT SQUASH QUEEN HEADS	Vegan	Use a vegan butter substitute.
SWEET OR SAVORY ROASTED PURPLE SWEET POTATO	Paleo	Only the savory variation of this dish is paleo.
KOREAN-INSPIRED SALMON CEVICHE	Paleo	Omit tomatoes.
MARINARA SAUCE	Halal	Omit balsamic vinegar
ORANGE-CRANBERRY SAUCE	Paleo	Substitute maple syrup for brown sugar; omit white sugar and rum.
	Halal	Omit rum.

CONVERSION CHART

VOLUME

IMPERIAL	CUPS	METRIC
-	¼ tsp	1.25ml
-	½ tsp	2.5ml
-	1 tsp	5ml
-	1 Tbsp	15ml
3 ½ fl oz	-	100ml
4 ½ fl oz	½ cup	125ml
5 fl oz	-	150ml
7 fl oz	-	200ml
9 fl oz	1 cup	250ml
11 fl oz	-	300ml
14 fl oz	-	400ml
18 fl oz	2 cups	500ml
26 fl oz	3 cups	750ml
35 fl oz	4 cups	1L
53 fl oz	6 cups	1.5L
70 fl oz	8 cups	2L

WEIGHT

IMPERIAL	METRIC
½ oz	15g
1 oz	30g
2 oz	60g
3 oz	85g
4 oz (¼ lb)	115g
5 oz	140g
6 oz	170g
7 oz	200g
8 oz (½ lb)	230g
16 oz (1 lb)	450g
32 oz (2 lb)	950g
35 oz (2 ⅕ lb)	1kg

TEMPERATURE

FAHRENHEIT	CELSIUS	GAS
250°F	120°C	½
275°F	140°C	1
300°F	150°C	2
325°F	160°C	3
350°F	180°C	4
375°F	190°C	5
400°F	200°C	6
425°F	220°C	7
450°F	230°C	8
475°F	240°C	9
500°F	260°C	10

LENGTH

IMPERIAL	METRIC
¼ in	6mm
½ in	13mm
1 in	25mm
2 in	51mm
1 ft	305mm
1 ft 8in	500mm
1 yard	915mm
3 ft 3 in	1000mm

ABOUT THE AUTHOR

Chris-Rachael Oseland is an Austin, Texas-based nerdy cookbook writer and personal chef. For lots of free nerdy recipes or to book her for your next event, visit KitchenOverlord.com

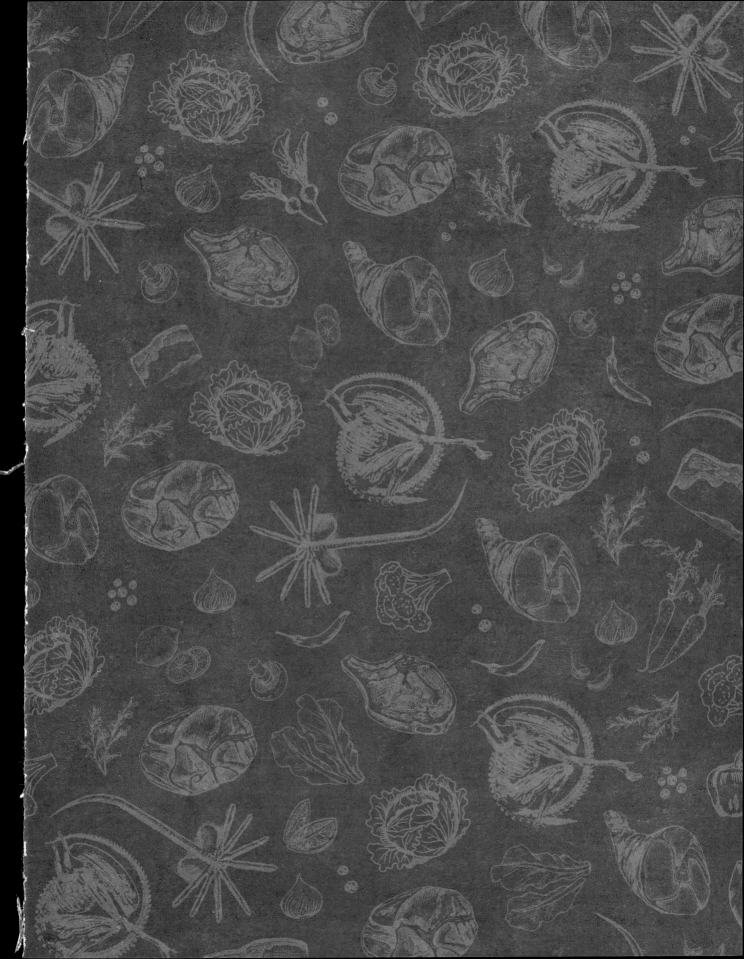

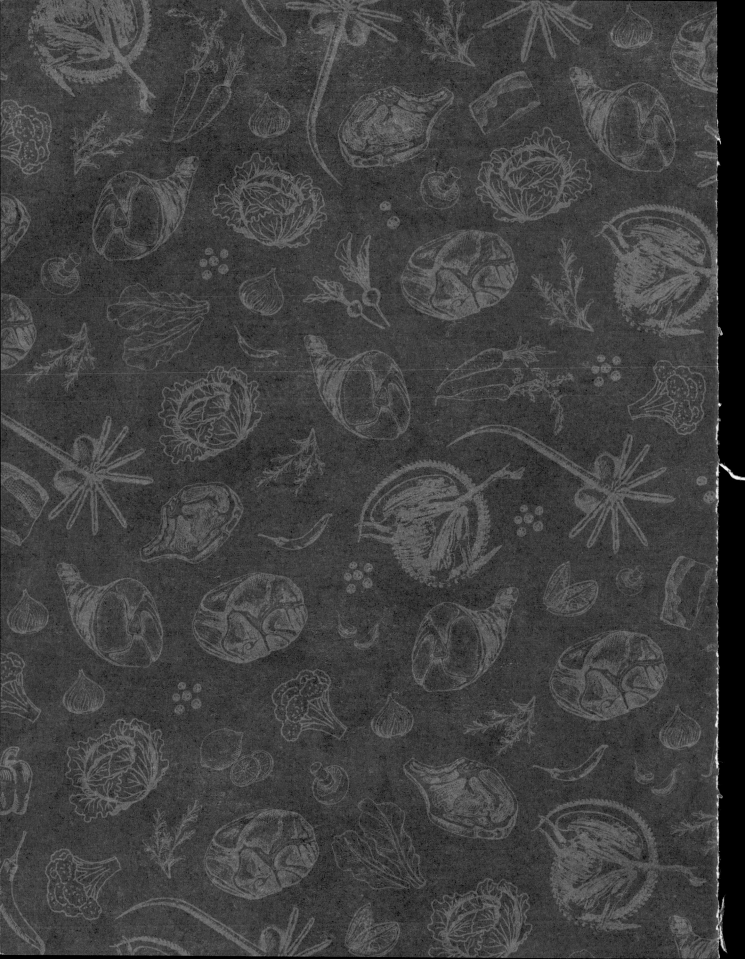